D1596745

LEOPOLDO ZEA

FROM *MEXICANIDAD* TO A PHILOSOPHY OF HISTORY

Solomon Lipp

The author analyzes Mexican national identity in the context of the philosophy of Leopoldo Zea, contemporary Mexican thinker. He attempts to establish national character traits peculiar to Mexico, using sociological, psychological, historical, and philosophical approaches. He then shows how Zea deals with the problem of Mexican identity and how he relates specifically Mexican concepts to universal philosophic and historic thought. Ranging widely over many disciplines, this scholarly study will be particularly valuable to readers familiar with philosophy, sociology, and psychology.

Solomon Lipp teaches in the Department of Hispanic Studies, McGill University. His numerous publications in the fields of foreign languages, literature, and philosophy include Three Chilean Thinkers *(WLU Press, 1975) and* Three Argentine Thinkers.

LEOPOLDO ZEA

FROM *MEXICANIDAD* TO A PHILOSOPHY OF HISTORY

Solomon Lipp

Canadian Cataloguing in Publication Data

Lipp, Solomon, 1913-
  Leopoldo Zea

Bibliography: p.
Includes index.

ISBN 0-88920-079-3

1. Zea, Leopoldo 1912-   — Addresses, essays,
lectures.   2. Philosophy, Mexican — Addresses,
essays, lectures.

B1019.Z434   199.72092'4   C80-094029-6

Copyright © 1980
WILFRID LAURIER UNIVERSITY PRESS
Waterloo, Ontario, Canada N2L 3C5

79 80 81 82 4 3 2 1

To Sylvia
once again
and
always

CONTENTS

PREFACE

The name Leopoldo Zea in the title of this work indicates that the original thrust of the study was primarily in the field of philosophy and the history of ideas. However, as the project progressed, it became evident that other disciplines would have to be brought into the picture. Since the principal themes of the study relate to such thorny problems as "Latin American" philosophy, "Mexican" attributes and "essence," it was thought best to attempt initially to arrive at an acceptable definition of terms. Within this framework the philosophical contributions of Leopoldo Zea are examined. The philosopher is placed within his historical circumstance: how does he view his country, his continent, his universe?

At the outset a series of questions present themselves, questions which urgently demand answers. Assuming the validity of the terms involved, what is meant by the "Mexican" or "Latin American" approach, as applied to philosophic study? What is Mexican "essence"? What are Mexican "traits"? Clearly, one cannot limit oneself to philosophic interpretation in an attempt to decipher the constellation of assumed characteristics. One must also have recourse to studies that have been realized in other disciplines as well, e.g., sociology and psychology.

The present volume, then, is an effort to achieve a synthesis. An attempt has been made to bring together several perspectives, all bearing on the same theme, namely, "Mexicanness,"[1] or the nature of Mexican "essence," "character," or "personality." Perhaps Mexico, more than any other country in the Western hemisphere, presents a vibrant example of *mestizaje*, together with all of its accompanying sociopsychological manifestations.

Attempts to delve into the Mexican "soul," to define and analyze his "being," may result in a highly frustrating experience. After examining the many efforts in this direction—in the fields of sociology, psychology and philosophy—one can only wonder whether, indeed, there *is a* Mexican character or personality, sufficiently uniform and homogeneous as to be applicable to all regions of the country, and valid for all classes of the population. "Character" or "personality" studies

---

[1] "Mexicanness," an awkward term at best, used to denote *Mexicanidad* or "lo mexicano," i.e., the total configuration of the qualities involved. The other possibility, "Mexicanism," is too limited for the purpose of this essay.

can be risky affairs. At best, they deteriorate too easily into delightful literary sketches, based on fleeting impressions, or else, in the worst of cases, ugly stereotypes which scarcely contribute to the cultural empathy one might be trying to achieve.[2] Then, too, the author of these lines perceived the possibility, on occasion, of becoming identified with his subject matter to such an extent as to be controlled by his findings, instead of the other way around. This danger he has studiously attempted to avoid.

From a philosophical perspective, any attempt to explore the so-called essence of "Mexicanness" implies an analysis of historical circumstances which have conditioned the nature of that essence. Within this historical framework it means an examination of the Mexican's existence, his behaviour as both subject and object. Introspective analysis is not enough. What matters are his actions and reactions in an historical context, a context which he has inherited and which he continues to fashion. "Essence," then, does not operate in a vacuum. It needs an "existence" thanks to which it may either develop or decay. Yet the converse is also true: existence needs an essence "to feed on." There can be no "pure" existentialism or historicism, divorced from essence.[3]

Furthermore, a number of vexatious complications arise when this exercise in Mexican essence is undertaken—regardless of the point of view, i.e., whether it be philosophical or sociological. One may well ask: Is the Mexican the *only* person sufficiently qualified to analyze himself and his reality? Is his the only valid approach? Can he, acting as both subject and object of his circumstance, produce a study which is, hopefully, objective and reliable? Is he not, perhaps, too deeply enmeshed in his own reality to be sufficiently dispassionate insofar as this is possible? On the other hand, if this study of Mexicanness is to partake of an "objective" quality, is it possible for a non-Mexican to embark upon a project of this kind? Assuming that this non-Mexican has had his

---

[2] The point bears repetition: no matter how much evidence may be adduced to substantiate an hypothesis, or regardless of the undeniable intellectual stature of the author in question, studies in characterology are bound to result in highly polemical treatises, and call forth no end of controversy, if not acrimony. See, for example, Geoffrey Gorer, *The American People: A Study in National Character* (New York: W. W. Norton, 1948), and Salvador Madariaga, *Englishmen, Frenchmen and Spaniards* (London: Oxford University Press, 1928). Gorer himself states that it is "difficult to make valid generalizations about nearly a hundred million people scattered over half a continent" (p. 15). Madariaga's intriguing study of national character makes the point that there is a definite attitude towards life which distinguishes a people. In the Englishman it is the spirit of *fair play*, in the Frenchman, the concept of *le droit*, and finally, in the Spaniard, the chief concern is *el honor*. Out of these responses are born action, thought, and passion respectively (pp. 4-8). Yet Madariaga admits that his assertions are based on an "hypothesis" and "some intuitional knowledge" (p. xviii)—this, in spite of the fact that he insists that "there is such a thing as national character" (p. xi).

[3] J. Gaos, *En torno a la filosofía mexicana*, vol. 2 (Mexico: Porrúa y Obregon, S.A., 1955), p. 47.

contacts with the Mexican scene in more than superficial fashion, can he bring to his study a relatively unbiased, fresh point of view?[4]

In recent decades research in psychology and sociology has been characterized by a refinement in techniques of investigation. Scholars in these fields have given us pilot studies on a limited scale—based on case studies and questionnaires—of various ethnic groups, including the Mexicans. Admittedly, these have concentrated on a rather restricted sampling of the population concerned (either geographically or socioeconomically). Yet they have, nevertheless, managed to offer certain insights (often based on so-called "scientific," quantitative evidence) into personality factors which can be said to be sufficiently persistent and repetitive, as to constitute a culture trait, peculiar to that particular group. Yet one must always bear in mind that not only are there regional differences which must be recognized whenever one undertakes a study of so-called national or ethnic characteristics. There are also differences within social groups residing in the same area. In any case, this type of study is supposedly more "valid" and "reliable" than the poetic insights, often characterized by great lyrical charm and beauty, which purport to describe the "essence" of a given people.[5] Authors who have dealt with this subject are always careful to avoid generalizations. Thus, Sania Hamady is quick to insert in the Preface:[6] "I have not taken just a full account of the changes that the Arab social system is undergoing. This is justified by the fact that these modifications in the Arab way of life, and therefore in the Arab character and behavior, are very slow and restricted mainly to the upper class and urban areas." Nevertheless, Hamady does not hesitate to add: "The character presented derives its source only from what is "common" among the Arabs, and therefore allows me to make merely simple generalizations." As an afterthought, and as though the author did not wish to appear vulnerable, the following assertion concludes the Preface: "My statements are not to be considered absolute or conclusive."

In the most positive sense, all that can be affirmed with some degree of validity is that certain characteristics, considered "typical" of a given group, are manifested by a significant number of members of that group. The only weakness here seems to lie in the absence of a definition of the term "significant." Is it to be defined from a statistical point of view? If so, what percentage of frequency of appearance must be encountered before a trait is considered "significant"? One might add that a national character trait may not—nor does it have to—be representative of the majority of the population.

[4] The subject of Mexicanness, considered by a qualified foreigner, is touched upon by Gaos, p. 78.

[5] See in this respect Octavio Paz, *El laberinto de la soledad* (3rd ed., Mexico: Fondo de Cultura Económica, 1963).

[6] Sania Hamady, *Temperament and Character of the Arabs* (New York: Twayne Publishers, 1960).

Erich Fromm presents the picture in sharper focus, distinguishing between "social character," which is shared by most members of the same culture, as distinct from "individual character," in which people belonging to the same culture differ from each other. The concept of social character is not statistical. It can be understood only in terms of its function. Fromm maintains that "society," in general, does not exist. Only specific social structures exist. These are relatively fixed at any given period, although they do experience change in the course of historical development. Members of various social groups, i.e., within these structures, behave in such a way as to be able to function effectively in the sense required by society as a whole. Social character thus shapes the energies of people. "People want to act as they have to act.... The social character has the function of moulding human energy for the purpose of the functioning of a given society."[7]

Erich Fromm's work is merely one outstanding example of the many psychoanalytic studies which deal with personality traits of various national groups. These studies have—in the case of our immediate interest—applied principles and methodology, borrowed from the field of depth psychology, in an attempt to shed light on certain Mexican "characteristics." As will be seen in the main body of the text, some of these interpretations are far from being the last word.

Central to the study undertaken in this volume is the work of Leopoldo Zea, one of Mexico's outstanding philosophers today. Zea headed a group of young intellectuals who, after the Second World War, concerned themselves with the specific nature of their country's possible contribution to philosophic thought. Eventually, Zea went beyond the geographic borders of Mexico, and delved into the possibility of a Latin American philosophical perspective, and its relationship to so-called universal themes. In attempting to speak of the Mexican component, Zea and his group found themselves constrained to define their terms of reference. As stated in the beginning of this Preface, they were faced by the question: What is "Mexican" from a philosophical point of view? In looking for the answer, they found inspiration and a possible point of departure in the Revolution of 1910 which had given powerful impetus to the resurgence of Mexican nationalism—resistance to domination by foreign interests and their local representatives. Rebellion and self-assertiveness, so obvious in the political and economic spheres, also extended to other fields of endeavour. Long-suppressed creativity seemed to burst forth in archaeological excavations, in painting, music, and literature. It was inevitable that the fever should extend also to the realm of philosophy and the history of ideas.

The philosophic framework, then, represents the main thrust of this essay. Additional material, gleaned from other disciplines, can be

---

[7] Erich Fromm, "Psychoanalytic Characterology and its Application to the Understanding of Culture," in *Culture and Personality*, ed. S. Stansfield Sargent and Marion W. Smith (New York: Viking Fund, 1949), pp. 4-5.

considered tangential, although certainly not unimportant. Zea himself was influenced by other thinkers, both in Mexico and abroad. The group which he directed was prolific in its treatment of the theme under consideration, although the results did not always attain the same high level of quality which distinguishes the writing of Zea himself.

The flurry of activity in this area seemed to subside as the decade of the fifties drew to a close. However, sociologists and psychologists—as opposed to philosophers—continued to concern themselves with the subject. Zea had already begun to expand his horizons to include the continent as a whole, and more specifically, the relationship, as he saw it, between Latin America and the Western World. An inevitable outgrowth of this enlarged and enriched perspective was the role which Latin America was to play—as he conceived it—with specific reference to the problems facing the nations of the Third World.

A considered judgment of Zea's contribution to Latin American thought cannot fail to include critical commentary which has appeared in both Mexican and foreign publications. Despite the fact that some of this criticism has, at times, been sharp and penetrating, it has always been marked by a profound respect for the high level of scholarship, characteristic of Zea's point of view. His constantly inquiring mind, his restless curiosity, and his apparently tireless search for answers to perplexing questions have called into being innumerable associations on the part of the author of this volume, and provoked in him the desire to venture into related fields of inquiry—all of which, as stated, is hopefully designed to yield a more comprehensive picture of this fascinating phenomenon, this sometimes irritating yet always elusive substance or process, known as the *ser mexicano*.

This book has been published with the help of a grant from the Canadian Federation for the Humanities, using funds provided by the Social Sciences and Humanities Research Council of Canada. In addition, I want to express my appreciation to the Council for a grant which enabled me to spend two summers in Mexico, in 1973 and 1974, to carry on the necessary research for this project. In this connection, I would also like to thank the Colegio de Mexico for making available its library facilities, without which my efforts would have been quite frustrated. Finally, as always, my deepest gratitude to my wife, Sylvia Ehrlich Lipp, who spent many long hours in the laborious task of preparing the manuscript.

INTRODUCTION

The search for identity, the attempt to define oneself—the result of the individual's sense of alienation—is not restricted to contemporary man alone; nor is it exclusively peculiar to the period of anguished questioning which follows the Second World War. It can also be applied to national groups, if not an entire continent. And it also goes back more than a century—at least in the case of Spanish America—to the period immediately following Independence from Spain. For it is during this period that a whole generation of Romantic liberals was inquiring into the very essence of the newly emancipated nations, and asking: Who are we? Questions which were the result of a sad realization on the part of these intellectuals, intoxicated by the rich wine of republican ideals, that Spanish America had been emancipated only in the political sense; intellectual independence was still a long way off.

Echeverría and Sarmiento in Argentina, Lastarria and Bilbao in Chile, Mora in Mexico—these were but a few of an impressively large group of leaders who rejected the colonial tradition of Spain, blaming it for the apparently endless chain of dictatorships, followed by chaos, only to be succeeded once again by military rule. In order to root out the evil effects of the Spanish heritage, it would be necessary to bring about a change in the mentality inherited from the mother country. Only then could Spanish America progress along the road to democratic government—something for which it was, at the moment, completely unprepared.

How was this to be realized? How could old customs be stamped out and new habits implanted? By education, industrial development, immigration. In what ways were these to be implemented? By imitation, by utilizing foreign models, by importing ideas, labour, and institutions from abroad.

Echeverría looked to the French utopian socialists for inspiration. Bilbao argued that there could be no reconciliation between Republicanism and Catholicism. "Let us be the United States of South America," exclaimed Sarmiento. "To govern is to populate," wrote Alberdi, as he urged an influx of European immigrants, especially Anglo-Saxon, since these were more industrious.

Thus were sown the seeds of what was bound to result in a never-ending conflict between the advocates of two points of view: those who would "Europeanize" or "North Americanize" in the name of "progress," and those who would defend the "traditional" and *criollo* values, in the name of preserving the "authenticity" of the Spanish American ethos.

The historical pendulum was to oscillate periodically; action was to provoke reaction. First one extreme, then the other: the conflict between the "modernizers," the "cosmopolites" on the one hand, and the "nativists" on the other; between "civilization" and "barbarism," "city" and "province," Buenos Aires and Cordoba.

The two component elements could, apparently, not be synthesized. They were mutually exclusive. The conflict expressed itself in social and economic terms; it was felt in politics and literature. Martin Fierro became the rallying cry of those who saw their "authentic" identity subverted. And yet those who had turned their backs on this sort of authenticity were themselves frustrated. The progress they had hoped to achieve as a result of having proclaimed the superiority of foreign models seemed to elude them. They had not found themselves.

The search and the self-analysis continued. The question of identity was still unanswered. But this time—a century later—in Mexico, Argentina, and other parts of the continent, the attempted examinations and dissections were more mature, the techniques of analysis more sophisticated. Not only history and literature, but also sociology, psychology, and philosophy were appealed to and utilized in an attempt to arrive at a more satisfactory solution of the problem, namely, the character of the Argentine, the Mexican, the Brazilian, etc. In fact, not only might one ask: What, for example, was the nature of "Mexicanness," but also, what was the image of Latin America as a whole vis-à-vis the rest of the world?

In specifically Mexican terms, why was there so much concern with the national or continental ethos in the first place? Perhaps the reason goes back to the conflict between Anglo-Saxonism and the Latin spirit, as this had been perceived by Rodó and Vasconcelos. These, as well as those that followed them, e.g., Alfonso Reyes and Pedro Henríquez Ureña, had viewed the continent in terms of a future hope and destiny for mankind. Ibero-American civilization, with all its defects, could turn out to be the model which would convert all men into a new type of human being. For Reyes, Latin America represented a hope for European man, a refuge for his freedom of conscience, and an opportunity to build a better world. "We are late arrivals at the banquet of European civilization," he had written in his *Ultima Tule*.[1] This continent had always been the dream of the discontented and the reformers, the radical optimists. Even in a geographic sense, the continent was "leftist," since, according to the map, Reyes asserted, one had to go left in travelling from Europe to America. Now that Mexico had come of age,

---

[1] Alfonso Reyes, *Ultima Tule*, in *Obras Completas*, vol. 11 (Mexico: Fondo de Cultura Económica, 1960), 82-83 (my translation, as are all others, unless otherwise indicated — S.L.).

Europe and the rest of the world would soon have to learn to "reckon with us" (p. 90).

In the eyes of the Mexicans, their country became identified with the continent, its promise and destiny, its possibilities and short-comings, crystallized and concentrated within its national boundaries; and its study and analysis a matter of national concern.

There was also another factor. The Mexican compared his culture with others, and as a result, realized that he was "different." Now there are several ways of dealing with such a realization. The first is to deny that any differences exist, especially if these cause feelings of discom-fort. In that case it is usually convenient to take refuge in the slogan that "we are all equal." Another solution is to imitate the norms and stan-dards of other cultures—a process which probably reinforces the orig-inal feelings of "differentness," inadequacy, or "inferiority." Finally, the third way out, the healthiest and most mature of all, is that of recognizing and accepting the existence of these differences, and dis-carding any sense of shame or fear. This implies searching out and analyzing the causes that make for such discomfort— if, indeed, the latter exists—and taking stock of one's cultural heritage. This is what is meant by the phrase, "acquiring awareness" of oneself. Perhaps it is no exaggeration to say that in no other Latin American country has this phenomenon been manifested in so acute a manner as in Mexico in the course of the past several decades.

The search for national awareness and identity became a central focus of attention, especially after the Mexican Revolution, for many statesmen, artists, and writers. Vasconcelos, for example, attempted a program of national education in an effort to raise the cultural level of the country, only to fail because it was just another "utopia." Neverthe-less, this very failure was the spark which stimulated others to confront Mexican reality rationally, in an attempt to resolve the manifold prob-lems facing the country. Even though the door to universalism had been opened, Mexican thinkers began to stress national values. For example, Antonio Caso appealed to the intellectuals to work out solu-tions in conformity with the national ethos, and disregard social theories which had their origin in Europe.[2] Samuel Ramos argued that it was necessary to turn one's attention to Mexican reality, and avoid a Europeanism based on a universal culture without roots in Mexico, as well as a "picturesque" Mexicanism without universality.[3] The solution, according to Ramos, lay in an adaptation of universal culture to Mex-ican reality. One must find the seed of overseas culture which might germinate in Mexican soil and yield the fruits applicable to the neces-

[2] Antonio Caso, *México: Apuntamientos de cultura patria* (Mexico: Imprenta Univer-sitaria, 1943), p. 20.
[3] Samuel Ramos, *El Perfil del hombre y la cultura en México* (5th ed., Mexico: Austral, 1972), pp. 90-91.

sities peculiar to that nation. But for this it was first essential to extirpate the Mexican's sense of inferiority which caused him to belittle his reality.

* * * * *

The attempt to define the identity and personality of Mexico, or for that matter of Latin America as a whole, was related intimately to the study of the history of ideas. It acquired sharpened focus on the continent as a result of the influence exerted by Ortega y Gasset during the first quarter of the present century, as well as the efforts on the part of his disciples, notably José Gaos. Latin American culture—its essence and value in relation to universal culture—could be studied and its meaning discovered only in terms of Ortega's "perspectivism," i.e., the historicist approach. This consisted in viewing man within the framework of his concrete situation, situated within a definite historical circumstance. Man—in this case Latin American or Mexican man—was not an abstraction; he was an individual peculiar unto himself and unlike anyone else.

Gaos was not the first to attempt to discover something "different," "original," or "authentic" in Mexican culture or essence. Justo Sierra, before him, had spoken of the cultural uniqueness of Mexico, and of the need for the country to develop in authentic fashion. But Gaos insisted that attempts to utilize philosophic concepts in order to explain Mexicanness could not be realized successfully in universal terms. Truth, for example, could not be understood as a manifestation of a universal reality, but rather as an expression of each individual's concrete reality. Hence, reality was not uniform, nor the same for all; it was always viewed from the individual's particular perspective.[4]

* * * * *

This approach carries with it the definite implication that each point of view is equally original by virtue of the fact that it expresses its own peculiar reality. However, not only do diverse circumstances—both temporal and spatial—make for different "truths," as historicism insists in its interpretation of a given culture. The individual's interests, aptitudes, and preferences also condition one's view of truth and reality. Gaos stressed this dual component in his discussion of Mexican "essence" and the possibility of developing an original philosophy of Mexicanness. It is to him, more than anyone else, that attempts to forge an authentic Mexican philosophy owe their greatest stimulation and impetus.

[4] See in this connection María de los Angeles Knockenhauer, "José Gaos y la Filosofía de lo Mexicano," *Revista de la Universidad de México* 24, no. 9 (May 1970), 22.

Lest the historicist approach be thought of as the equivalent of the narrowly relativistic point of view, the following consideration should be borne in mind. If philosophizing about Mexican quality, value, and essence is the result of the quest for identity, i.e., the attempt by Mexicans to overcome their lack of understanding and clarity about themselves, then it would seem to follow that this activity would cease when the historical circumstances which gave rise to this type of philosophizing would themselves be altered. In other words, philosophizing or agonizing about the Mexican is a stage in the cultural development of the country, a phase in the maturation process of national awareness. It follows that one of two alternatives becomes evident at this point: (1) If Mexican writers no longer seem concerned with the question, then the country will have progressed to a higher stage in its evolution; (2) If the intellectual activity continues along these lines, then that stage has, apparently, not yet been reached. Curiously enough and paradoxically perhaps, from the historicist point of view this philosophizing can be said to have been successful if it vanishes; its very disappearance is proof of its success (p. 26).

One would conclude from the above that from this vantage point philosophic truth can be viewed as historic not in a merely relativistic, i.e., fleeting sense, but rather as indicative of a process which strives to achieve improvement in the quality of thought and to perfect its functioning in accordance with the reality expressed. Truth is thus historic because it has to be demonstrated continually.

It should not seem surprising that José Gaos, the Spaniard, should concern himself with the problem of Mexican reality. Gaos, the refugee who made his home in Mexico after the triumph of Franco's forces, applied a philosophical yardstick in his analysis of the Mexican scene, similar to that utilized by the Generation of 1898 in its analysis of Spain's condition. The writers of the Generation had also shown great concern for Spain and its essence, its ills, the causes thereof, and the possible solutions. They too had delved into Spanish reality—no matter how depressing—in order to study its historical destiny and seek its salvation.

In the same way that Spain had seemed "marginal" to the rest of Europe, Latin America, too, was marginal and had to examine itself in order to find ways and means of achieving integration with the rest of the world community. Mexico especially, aided by Gaos, attempted to formulate a philosophy of national ethos.

The question of Mexican philosophy in particular, and of Latin American philosophy in general, has since given rise to endless polemics. Yet Gaos was certainly not the first to deal with the subject. As far back as the mid-nineteenth century, the Argentinian Juan Bautista Alberdi had proclaimed the necessity for such a philosophy. There was no Latin American philosophy, he had complained, but there should be one. The continent was content to feed on foreign, imported models; it was satisfied with imitations. America had always practised what Europe was thinking. However each country, each age, had offered different solutions to the problem of the human spirit. Philosophy was nationalized by its specific application to the needs of each country at a given moment. There had been philosophy in, but not of, Latin America.

Nowhere does the conflict between national orientation and universal values appear more evident than in these discussions concerning Latin American thought. Alberdi's compatriot, Alejandro Korn, was to affirm half a century later that philosophy ought to be oriented toward the treatment of problems involved in national development, yet without losing sight of the universal human dimension.

José Vasconcelos took another tack. Attempting to transcend the dichotomy, he asserted that America was capable of surpassing Europe in the realm of thought. Universality was itself characteristic of Latin America. Nevertheless, the national component seemed to emerge triumphant. The continent was heir to all of the experiences which Europe and Asia had to offer, since it had always been the crossroads of the world. Even though Vasconcelos seemed opposed to universalism, he was, nevertheless, careful to distinguish between philosophic nationalism and a philosophy which was forged as a result of national experience. We can lay claim to a philosophy from the Hispanic point of view, he insisted, with the same right that Germans, Frenchmen, or Englishmen have to their respective national schools. These are all considered points of departure in an effort to elevate humanity.[5]

Antonio Caso had also rejected imitation of foreign models. Let us stop imitating—he wrote—the political-social regimes of Europe. Mexico cannot continue to assimilate the attributes of others. Its miseries, its revolutions, its tragic bitterness are the fruits of imitation.[6]

On the other hand, one should not judge too harshly. Something had to be imitated. Foreign models did cross the Atlantic. They could not be kept out. The first philosophy, for example, was brought over by the Spaniards. What is important to bear in mind is that European philosophies acquired a different nuance upon arrival.

Nevertheless, the contemporary Peruvian philosopher, Salazar Bondy, believes that it is precisely this influx of ideas over a period of more than four centuries, this adoption of foreign models, which has resulted in considerable intellectual frustration. The world at large does not react to the thinking of Latin Americans. The very question raised as to the existence of a Latin American philosophy is merely symptomatic of this difficulty.[7] The main thrust of Salazar Bondy is

[5] José Vasconcelos, *Etica* (Madrid: Aguilar, 1932), p. 25.
[6] Antonio Caso, p. 29.
[7] Augusto Salazar Bondy, *¿Existe una filosofía de nuestra América?* (Mexico: Siglo XXI Editores, S.A., 1968), pp. 41-42.

that Latin America will not be able to create an authentic philosophy until it emerges from its present level of underdevelopment.[8]

It might be pointed out in this connection that Gaos, too, had maintained that national philosophies do not appear until the respective nations are formed on a sound basis. This implies overcoming economic difficulties inherent in underdevelopment. Culture and nationhood, then, appear to be functions of social and economic progress. We therefore seem to be faced by a contradiction. On the one hand, Latin American thinkers are urged to create philosophy. On the other, it is stated that Latin America is still underdeveloped—a condition which would preclude philosophizing.

Despite this apparent inconsistency, Gaos insisted that philosophizing about one's historical circumstances would result in something really original and creative. Applied to the Mexican scene, one may argue, as does the contemporary Mexican philosopher, Abelardo Villegas, that the history of a people indeed constitutes its very essence, and that all attempts to speak in terms of a peculiarly Mexican philosophy or a philosophy of Latin American "essence" are merely idle lucubrations, the result of an exaggerated sense of nationalism.[9] While it is true that Gaos admitted that there is as yet no American philosophy, as opposed to a European philosophy, there is, nevertheless, a desire to see one brought into being. It is not so much a question of developing an *American* or *Spanish* philosophy. It is more important that Americans, Spaniards, Mexicans, Argentinians, etc., simply create philosophy—a point which was to be stressed subsequently by Leopoldo Zea. Moreover, this philosophy should include a study of the sociohistorical context of the people in accordance with Ortega's doctrine of circumstantiality. It is therefore important for the Mexican, for example, to take stock of his position in the world. This will surely result in contact with European currents of thought.[10] One may well be tempted to ask at this point: Why is it that Latin America has developed a literature of such outstanding quality, especially since the Second World War, if cultural phenomena cannot flourish because of underdevelopment? Perhaps it would be more accurate to say that the interconnectedness between philosophy and historical circumstance has in the case of Latin America given rise, not to philosophy per se, but to political philosophy, philosophy of education, philosophy of history—in short, philosophy in problem areas, precisely because of conditions of underdevelopment and/or national integration.

* * * * *

[8] Ibid., p. 126.
[9] Abelardo Villegas, "José Gaos y la filosofía hispanoamericana," *Revista de la Universidad de México* 24, no. 9 (May 1970), 11.
[10] Salazar Bondy, p. 77.

Gaos, then, had his precursors, when he arrived in Mexico. Without denying the value of his contributions, it should be said that he also had his contemporaries who were taking their initial steps in the direction of explaining and interpreting Mexican consciousness. One of these was the young Mexican philosopher, Samuel Ramos, who initiated a significant change of emphasis in philosophic attitudes. One writer has maintained that there was a parallel between the role exercised by Ortega in Spain and that of Ramos in Mexico.[11] The latter, too, was influenced by philosophic currents emanating from Germany. Ramos reflected upon the crisis in humanism, and attempted an investigation into Mexican culture by examining Mexico's past record in philosophy. The Mexicans had developed their culture chiefly by imitating nineteenth-century Europe, especially France. Culturally and spiritually, Mexico was still a colonial country.[12] The reason for this was twofold: (1) The country suffered from a feeling of inferiority which had its origin in the period of conquest and colonization; (2) Political and social instability impeded cultural development and frustrated all efforts on the part of Mexico to define itself.

Mimetismo or imitation led to self-denigration and escape to Europe in order to become "cultured." But this was definitely not the way to create Mexican culture. A reaction was bound to set in. The First World War had left a spirit of pessimism and disillusion in its wake. Spengler, too, had contributed to the decrease in admiration for the West. The result was a turning inward upon oneself, a realization of the need for introspective examination. On the other hand, the Revolution of 1910 had kindled national sentiment; xenophobia was on the increase.

Ramos warned against both extremes. Rejecting European values and attempting, consequently, to create a Mexican utopia out of nothing was as bad as denying Mexican reality and donning a European mask. Yet one could not turn one's back on Europe. Isolation was not the answer. It was impossible to build Mexican culture by erasing universal history.

In short, "nationalists" as well as "Europeanizers" were mistaken in their approach vis-à-vis the forging of a national culture. Nationalists would isolate Mexico from the rest of the world. Instead of fostering the development of an authentic national spirit, this sort of attitude would destroy the spirit, authentic or otherwise. On the other hand, Europeanizers made the mistake of viewing Mexico through European eyes, and not vice versa (pp. 86-87). For Ramos, as well as for Latin Americans in general, philosophy offered not only a conception of the world and of life in general. It also served as a means of revealing *their*

[11] Rubén Salazar Mallén, *Samuel Ramos* (Mexico: Secretaría de Educación Pública, 1968), p. 20.
[12] Ramos, pp. 19-21.

world (i.e., the Latin Americans') and *their* life to them, and of showing them the position which *they* occupied in the world community.

The term "cultural derivation" was not evil in itself. Clearly, one had to distinguish between imitation or transplantation, and assimilation (p. 29). Imitation led to a false and negative profile of culture. On the other hand, assimilation was authentic and positive. It involved the adaptation of values taken from Western culture, values which were capable of being absorbed into the Mexican perspective and which would contribute to the formation of the national ethos. In order to develop our culture, we must "continue learning European culture. Our race is a ramification of a European race. Our history has developed within the European framework" (pp. 95-96). In short, maintained Ramos, what is called for is a blending of the specifics of the national character with values of a "universal" nature, or what may be referred to as the "Mexicanization of universal culture."

Since cultural evolution depends upon the nature of the Mexican, Ramos takes the next logical step: it becomes necessary to analyze the Mexican "psyche." Ramos' examination of the Mexican character, based on Adlerian psychology, is too well known to merit more than a brief summary of its salient points. The Mexican invents artificial goals which he can never attain, because he does not take into account his limitations, i.e., his reality. He plans as though he could choose anything he desires, regardless of historical or biological conditions. This causes him inevitably to imitate and to fail when the imitation does not turn out as expected. As a result, he attributes the blame for failure to the object imitated, rather than to his own limitation. Imitation has been a pattern of behaviour since Independence. This has produced, in turn, a series of negative personality characteristics: the Mexican is lacking in confidence in himself and in others; he is constantly irritable, on the defensive, and belligerent in order to bolster his ego; he seeks refuge in a world of fancy, is incapable of self-criticism, and must feel that others are always inferior. His ego must be nourished by human victims. He is explosive, intensely individualistic and undisciplined, and hence, indifferent to the welfare of the group. Ramos prefaces his remarks with the reassuring note that the Mexican is really not inferior; he merely thinks he is. This is a collective illusion (pp. 50-65).

The origin of this sense of inferiority is to be found in the contacts between the indigenous population and the Spanish Conquistador. The former was overwhelmed by the military machine of the invader. A second component was embedded in the nature of colonial society. The Spaniard was not a worker; he had no need to work since there were masses of Indians that could be exploited. Besides, had not his heritage dictated that work was beneath his dignity? Wealth was the result of exploitation of the lower classes. Only a few privileged individuals were able to derive the benefits of an education. The great mass was reduced to inactivity and poverty. Such a state of affairs was not conducive to the formation of a strong Mexican character.

After Independence had been won, Mexico wanted to be like Europe—all at once, in one great leap, so to speak—but was woefully unprepared to make the transition. Thus, the country was faced with a huge gap between ideals and realistic possibilities; between what the Mexican wanted to realize and what he was actually able to achieve. His abilities were inadequate to the task. The result was a strengthening of his sense of inferiority. Additional blows came in the form of war against the United States and the loss of Texas, French intervention, and the Maximilian episode. The Porfirio Díaz dictatorship favoured only those in power. Self-abasement was the result.

Yet Ramos ends on a positive note. It is necessary to change the image which the Mexican has of himself. He must remove the mask which hides his real identity. This can only be done via education. Perhaps what is needed is to practise the Socratic dictum of "know thyself" (p. 65). Only in a spirit of self-criticism can human personality be further developed.

Ramos' basic premise is open to question. One wonders whether the Adlerian concept of inferiority complex, applied to individual psychology, can be equally valid when an entire national group is evaluated. Another point of criticism is brought out by the contemporary philosopher, Basave Fernández del Valle. If the Mexican is the object of psychoanalysis, how can another Mexican, namely Ramos, be the psychoanalyst?[13] Basave Fernández del Valle notes that he does not believe in the existence of a specifically Mexican philosophy. "All attempts to build a Mexican philosophy have merely amounted to psychological and cultural anthropology." Our philosophy, insofar as it partakes of universal values, should, however, retain its characteristically Mexican overtones.[14]

Still another commentary comes from the pen of a contemporary critic who complains that Ramos erred in attributing the Mexican's sense of inferiority to the nation's history. What he should have done, instead, was to investigate the lives of individual Mexicans, or the development of the inferiority complex, as a clinical psychologist would have done.[15] The Mexican's inferiority complex is due not so much to the imposition of alien cultures, as Ramos would have us believe, but rather to "internally generated invidious processes" (p. 200).

Nevertheless, no matter what the shortcomings in Ramos' approach may be, one fact remains certain: his attempted formulation of

[13] Agustíin Basave Fernández del Valle, *Samuel Ramos* (Mexico: Universidad de Nuevo León, 1965), p. 32.

[14] Ibid., p. 30.

[15] Carl E. Batt, "Mexican Character: An Adlerian Interpretation," *Journal of Individual Psychology* 25, no. 2 (November 1969), 185.

the problem of Mexicanness, both in philosophical and psychological terms, stimulated further inquiry and analysis. Those who followed him continued to explore the problem, and eventually brought forth new postulates or revised old ones. Regrettably, Ramos never presented his readers with a definite scale of values with which to judge Mexican culture—a scale that would explain adequately the supposed sense of inferiority.[16]

Finally, one may well ask in this context: Is the application of Adlerian psychology to the Mexican scene a case of the tail wagging the dog? One may utilize a psychological doctrine in order to explain the Mexican. But one may also run the risk of inverting the process. In the first case, we may, possibly, trust the instrument; in the second, we may be deluding ourselves to the extent that we are trying to find in the Mexican elements to justify the formulations contained in the theory.

[16] Abelardo Villegas, *La filosofía de lo mexicano* (Mexico: Fondo de Cultura Económica, 1960), p. 133.

CHAPTER ONE

THE
PSYCHOLOGICAL APPROACH

In the Preface of the first volume of the series entitled *México y lo mexicano*[1] which he edited in the fifties, Leopoldo Zea remarked that the intellectual climate of the country was propitious for the study of the Mexican spirit and essence. Philosophers were beginning to turn away from abstract speculation and directing their attention to reflections concerning reality. Historians were probing the meaning of Mexican history; sociologists, psychologists, and literary critics were likewise engaged in applying the techniques of their disciplines to the national circumstance in an attempt to increase self-knowledge.

Yet this point of view, i.e., analyzing one's essence, was not without its opponents. The renowned Spanish philosopher, Eduardo Nicol, who migrated to Mexico after the Civil War, doubted strongly whether the essence of man in general, let alone that of the Mexican, could be defined. At best, variations peculiar to the Mexican simply constituted an accident or particular deviation from the universal "essence," that is, if one were to accept the hypothesis of such an essence in the first place. It would be more valid to speak of the Mexican's *manner* of being, rather than the being itself. The latter does not exist. Only human history exists.[2] In short, there is only a manner in which the human being can be said to function, a manner which produces different forms of existence. Man's structure is therefore conditioned and becomes evident in the course of his history (pp. 249-50).

Let it not be supposed that Samuel Ramos' psychological study was the first of its kind. At the beginning of this century there were at least two attempts made to define Mexican characterology. The studies are marked by an absence of sophisticated research techniques and, consequently, reveal the ever-present danger of stereotyped characterization, both positive and negative.

In 1901, for example, Julio Guerrero undertook an analysis of the Mexican character. Although he limited his study to the inhabitants of

[1] Alfonso Reyes, *La x en la frente* (Mexico: Porrúa y Obregón, 1952).
[2] Eduardo Nicol, "Meditación del propio ser," *Filosofía y letras* 20, no. 4 (October-December 1950), 248.

the central plateau, he stated that his findings could be extended to include the whole of Mexico. In his conclusion he found the following traits to be typical: lack of will, dishonesty, cruelty, melancholy, a tendency to scoff, and finally, the belief in chance.[3]

Guerrero attributed these psychological defects to the geographical conditions prevalent in the central plateau: the steep elevation above sea level, the rarity of the atmosphere, including its sudden and extreme changeability, and the arid landscape. All of these factors, he asserted, contribute to influence the physiology, psychology, character, culture, and industry of the Mexicans who inhabit this area (p. 352).

In the same year Ezequiel Chávez arbitrarily divided the Mexican population into four categories: Indian, creole, "superior" mestizo, and "ordinary" (vulgar) mestizo. Limiting himself to only one personality variable, namely sensitivity, Chávez concluded that the Indian was sluggish; his sensitivity was slow to respond to stimuli. This was due to the fact that he refused to break with his former culture patterns and accept the "civilizing influences" of the new culture (p. 329). On the other hand, the creole (and the European) is extremely sensitive. The "superior" mestizo is only moderately so, and has therefore been able to resist political turbulence more effectively than the "ordinary" mestizo who exhibits a more "variable" degree of sensitivity. This would also explain the ease with which the "ordinary" mestizo engages in amorous exploits; the family units he establishes are ephemeral (p. 330).

Family relationships and sexual mores, as a key to an understanding of the Mexican character, are discussed in numerous works— especially in the more recent decades—by psychologists and sociologists. These inevitably resort to history, both colonial and pre-Conquest, in order to explain the personality configuration (more often than not anti-social in nature).

Most of the studies make the point, as did Ramos in 1934, that Mexicans have to accept their ethnic origins, together with their positive and negative aspects. The latter must be analyzed, and once their existence is recognized, they should be destroyed by means of a rational approach.[4] One might wish to question this assumption, or indeed, doubt the possibility of its realization. It is one thing to recognize that these psychological defects exist, and quite another to *want* to get rid of them. This is essentially the same type of criticism that was made when Ramos' study appeared, in which he optimistically advanced the Socratic dictum, "Know thyself." We have learned quite a bit since Socrates, and even since Ramos! Enough to be able to say that in far too many cases, the individual guards his complexes jealously. He is actually in

[3] Juan Hernández Luna, "Primeros estudios sobre el mexicano en nuestro siglo," *Filosofía y Letras* 20, no. 4 (October-December 1950), 341-48.

[4] See, for example, Jorge Segura Millán, *Diorama de los mexicanos* (Mexico: B. Costa-Amic, 1964).

love with his neuroses and is afraid to part with them, since they afford him a much-needed measure of emotional security.

Almost all the psychological contributions considered in this study take as a point of departure the culture clash between the native population and the Spanish Conquistadores, and the resultant psychic manifestations. Two opposing views of the universe were bound to exert a traumatic effect upon the psyche of the newly-created racial type—the mestizo.

The introspective, self-analytical process, suggests Ramírez,[5] had to probe deeply into historical antecedents. This involved not only an examination of the culture conflict occasioned by the arrival of the Spaniards. It must also be borne in mind that prior to the Conquest, Mexico and Central America were populated by groups of people that were far from homogeneous in their composition. Serious tensions existed—the result of linguistic, political, and military differences. One group would impose its will upon the others. New cultural values absorbed and replaced former patterns of conduct. Nor should it be forgotten that in addition to the friction between one cultural-linguistic group and another, there were also social differences within each group. The unstable equilibrium was a constant factor. It changed only to the extent that the diverse groups would unite at a propitious moment to unseat the dominant group. The new conqueror would then continue in power under similar conditions of instability, until he, too, would be toppled (p. 33).

The sociopolitical picture was further complicated by the religious factor. The predominantly aggressive character of pre-Spanish Mexico was counterbalanced by the more benign value system, personified in the myth of Quetzalcóatl. Alfonso Caso refers to Quetzalcóatl as the benefactor of humanity who created man with his own blood, made possible his continued existence on earth through the discovery of corn, and taught him various arts and crafts.[6] Native mythology represents Quetzalcóatl as being engaged in a constant war with his enemy Texcatlipoca, the spirit of evil. This is reflected on the cosmic plane as the struggle between day and night. Good and Evil are thus identified with sunrise and sunset, or East and West.

The coming of the Spaniard had a dual effect insofar as the native population was concerned. In the first place, the dominant theocratic-military class saw in the Conquistador a threat to its power. Then, too, it interpreted his arrival in the New World in theological terms: Quetzalcóatl, in the person of the Spaniard, had re-appeared; he had come from the East. The tangible evidence of this belief inspired fear and panic in the ruling class, especially when it beheld the

[5] Santiago Ramírez, *El Mexicano: psicología de sus motivaciones* (8th ed., Mexico: Editorial Pax, 1972).

[6] Alfonso Caso, *El pueblo del sol,* Colección Popular (Mexico: Fondo de Cultura Económica, 1971), p. 39.

Spaniard's steed and experienced the effects of his use of gunpowder. As far as the submerged elements of the population were concerned, the Conquistador represented the hope of liberation from the yoke of the native military clique.[7]

Both factors were utilized by the Spaniards. One might venture the opinion that the objective conditions inherent in the native picture—the mythical imagery, the supernatural value system—were more instrumental in facilitating the Conquest than the subjective forces themselves, i.e., the military prowess of the Spaniards. In short, the image which the Indian projected upon the Spaniard was what defeated him. The pragmatic and realistic world of sixteenth-century Spain vanquished the mythical and magical world of the native. When the indigenous world, both exploiter and exploited, realized that the Conquistadores were neither a threat nor a hope, it was too late.

The Mexican's attempt, then, to find a national identity and define his character takes its point of departure in many studies, as was the case in Ramos' pioneering effort—in the Spanish Conquest, the crushing of indigenous culture, and subsequent instances of humiliation by foreigners.

The traumatic experience of the Conquest suffered by the indigenous population affected the relationship between men and women. The native Indian woman was plunged violently into a cultural situation for which she was totally unprepared, namely, being forced to minister to the biological needs of the Conqueror. The resultant union placed her in a position which might be considered a betrayal of her original culture. Ramírez, for example, claims that the birth of her son was the expression of her alienation from one world, but not an open door to another (p. 48). Hence, the woman, being the object of conquest, was viewed negatively. Her value as a human being plummeted to the extent that she was identified with the native population. Conversely, the value attributed to the man, i.e., the Spaniard, was exaggerated because he was identified with the Conqueror.

Octavio Paz has described this condition in poetic, although painful, terms: "The women are inferior beings because, on surrendering themselves, they open up. Their inferiority is constitutional . . . their wound never heals. . . . Every opening of our [masculine] being entails a diminution of our manliness."[8] The ideal represented by this manliness is never to break down, never to confide. The world in which the Mexican functions is a dangerous place. Suspicion of everything the world has to offer leads to hermeticism and scepticism. Paz's keen insights are well known, not only for their penetrating analysis, but also for their lyrical beauty. Dissimulation and irony, Paz goes on to say, are devices used by subjected peoples who disguise themselves in the

[7] Ramírez, p. 36.
[8] Octavio Paz, *El laberinto de la soledad* (4th ed., Mexico: Fondo de Cultura Económica, 1964), pp. 25-26.

presence of the master. Such subjugated groups always wear a mask, since the servant can only be himself in solitude (pp. 59-60). Although Paz grants a certain degree of validity to the historical explanation of Mexican behaviour patterns, he believes this interpretation to be insufficient. The wealthy classes also, not only the servant, shut themselves off from the external world. "Our attitude towards life is not conditioned by historical events, at least in the rigorous fashion that the speed or direction of a projectile is determined in the world of mechanics by a cluster of known factors. Our vital attitude . . . is also history" (p. 60). In other words, historical events are coloured by humanity which is always problematical. A reciprocal relationship exists between the two. Historical circumstances explain the Mexican character to the extent that this character explains the circumstances. Referring once more to the master-servant analogy, Paz maintains that although the servant is victimized by an outside power, a concrete reality, the Mexican, on the other hand, struggles against imaginary phantoms within himself, which prevent him from being himself. It is true that in some cases these phantoms have their origin in the Conquest; however, in others they reflect present-day problems. In either case, they have become divorced from their causes, and have assumed an independent existence (pp. 61-62).

Nevertheless, the Conquest and its resultant culture clash constitute the background within which Mexican intellectuals, as a group, find the origin of such traits of national character as inferiority and inadequacy, together with compensatory mechanisms, in the form of duplicity, aggression, and *machismo*. Jorge Carrión, too, refers to the conflict between the magical reality of the Indian and the rigorously logical constructs of the Spaniards. The former is forced to accept Catholicism as a means of escape from brutal reality. It will have to do in the face of psychological paralysis and sociological trauma, experienced as a result of the Conquest.[9] And into this painful world a loveless child is born, the mestizo, the result of violence, who experiences the conflict between magic and science; a marginal being in whose ambivalent subconsciousness the Spaniard represents force, authority, order, and pain, and the Indian, passivity and submission. A pathetic figure for whom Spain symbolizes the despotic, virile father figure, as opposed to the protection and tenderness of the Indian mother. This same mestizo, thus torn asunder inwardly by these conflicting elements, shouts *Viva México!* on holidays, is unable to explain the Spanish component of his origins, and refers contemptuously to the rural labourer as Indian (p. 113).

The mestizo can perhaps be said to represent a classic example of the sociological concept known as marginality. The marginal personal-

---

[9] Jorge Carrión, *Mito y magia del mexicano* (3rd ed., Mexico: Porrúa y Obregón, 1971), p. 12.

ity is the result of culture conflict, and suffers personal maladjustment in the process. The case can become pathological if accommodation or adjustment is not achieved. If the cultural differences include "sharp contrasts in race, and if the social attitudes are hostile, the problem of the individual whose sentiments are bound up with both societies, may well be acute."[10] In short, the marginal man is poised between the two worlds. Psychologically uncertain as a result, he often reflects the positive and negative elements of both. One of these usually dominates the other. The resultant form of attempted psychological integration to attain security is either assimilation into the dominant culture or nationalism of the subservient group. However, of late the Mexican mestizo seems to have transcended this formula. Representing a synthesis of the two antagonistic elements, he has developed a nationalism of his own, since he constitutes a majority of the population. Yet the two elements continue to do battle occasionally within his conscious and subconscious worlds.

Again, religious symbolism cannot be ignored in this respect. It, too, plays its role in the psychological interpretation of the Mexican's view of social relations as well as of himself. In historical terms, Quetzalcóatl, the creative, civilizing God of precolonial Mexico, the most human of all gods, the father principle, was replaced by the Holy Trinity of the Spaniards. Quetzalcóatl was thrust into the level of the subconscious. Yet the Mexican Indian, in order to bear up more effectively under the impact of the violent transformation of his reality, sought refuge in the feminine principle. Perhaps this would explain the metamorphosis of the Virgin Mary into the Virgin of Guadalupe, "the antithesis of Quetzalcóatl."[11]

Contemporary social relationships, especially within the family, the object of many sociological studies, also have their psychological explanation—again supported by the background of historical events. For example, the behaviour of the Spanish father of colonial times toward the Indian woman, in a sexual context, is reflected in the attitude of the adolescent youth today vis-à-vis the family maid. In both cases a feeling of arrogance and contempt exists side by side with physical violation. The feeling of male superiority has given an unfortunate, centuries-old coloration to marital relations in Mexican society. One of the outstanding characteristics in this respect is intense conflict between the sexes. Fatherless families are numerous. In other situations where the father uses economic power as a weapon of control, there is little love or affection. The woman, in turn, avenges herself by converting her children into instruments to be utilized against her husband. The son's exaggerated masculinity, or *machismo*, merely con-

[10] Everett V. Stonequist, *The Marginal Man: A Study in Personality and Culture Conflict* (New York: Charles Scribner's Sons, 1937), p. 3.

[11] Carrión, p. 49.

ceals an excessive dependence on his mother. The daughter, on the other hand, turns out to be a woman incapable of loving a man because of a basic distrust instilled in her, beginning with childhood.

In most cases the colonial Spaniard remained completely unconcerned as to the welfare of his illegitimate offspring. In fact many *peninsulares* sent home for Spanish women. These supposedly represented the idealized "spiritual" principle, in contrast to the "carnal" force, personified by the Indian woman. The importation of Spanish wives further complicated the sociopsychological picture. Spanish children born in the New World were faced, on the one hand, by a mother, highly refined and greatly esteemed, but very much engrossed in the social and religious activities of the day, and hence removed from the emotional needs of the child, and on the other hand, by the Indian maid who satisfied these needs, and provided warmth and comfort, but who was nevertheless considered inferior.[12] Thus the surrogate mother who offered affection was held in low esteem, thereby giving rise to psychological conflicts in the personality configuration of the child.[13]

As has been pointed out, the ambivalence which is characteristic of the mestizo in the cultural sense, i.e., Spanish versus Indian, also presents the conflict between the male and female principles, i.e., the attraction to the feminine image (which explains the cult of the Virgin of Guadalupe) and the yearning for the powerful father image. At the same time there is an ambivalence with respect to the father image itself, since the mestizo offspring of colonial Mexico both idealized and resented his Spanish father.

At an early age the father-figure becomes internalized in the Mexican boy. According to Ramírez, the origin of the male's predatory sexual activities is his desire to imitate the powerful Spaniards. We are faced here with an attempt to explain the social and cultural adjustment of the mestizo—or lack thereof—in sexual terms. If, for example, the mestizo attempts to become "creolized," (i.e., he assumes the culture patterns of the creole or "pure white" class which he emulates), he tends to conceal or deny his origins. Whereas the creole is proud of his antecedents, the mestizo, by contrast, tries to forget his past. His constant feeling of insecurity will cause him to act in servile fashion in the presence of his "betters."

If, on the other hand, he fails for whatever reason to achieve "creolization," and continues as a mestizo, his conflict will be of a different sort. In this case he is neither fish nor fowl; he has rejected his

----

[12] Ramírez, p. 51.

[13] This conflict of identity vis-à-vis "maid-mother" is not restricted to the Mexican scene. Guatemala, for example, is also a case in point, where an interesting sidelight may be observed. Children from well-to-do families, with excellent educational opportunities, will speak a substandard Spanish, due to the many years of intimate association with the lower-class maid, rather than the better-educated mother.

Indian heritage and has not been accepted by the creole world. As a result, he vents his hostility against the father-image. All of his pent-up emotions, acquired in childhood, burst forth. His desire to be strong like his father is matched by his hatred for him. The father has all this time maintained a minimum of contact with the family, and has, perhaps, rejected his son out of a sense of guilt. In many instances he has abandoned his family completely in favour of another family group (*la casa chica*). The mother, passive, long-suffering, and considered inferior, will be the prototype of the woman whom the son will marry eventually. She will, likewise, be mistreated in a show of male "superiority." The *machismo* of the son, as well as of his father before him, both in action and speech, is in the last analysis nothing but a symptom of the insecurity which underlies his masculinity. It is his "baroque expression of virility" (p. 62). Incidentally, this syndrome would also serve to explain his occasional outbursts of xenophobia. When the mestizo, for example, attacks the *gringo*, whom he incidentally admires and would like to imitate, he is, in reality, striking out at "absentee" masculinity, symbolized by the father, the chief target of his aggression.

As concerns the mother, the child evinces ambivalent feelings as well. On the one hand, he adores her; on the other, he hates her because somehow he holds her responsible for the fact that the father is never home. His hostility toward her increases when she casts him forth from the protective shelter of the home, probably because of the arrival of a new brother or sister. Conversely, the mother is overly possessive of the child as long as he is with her, because of her need to compensate for the absence of the husband (pp. 85-87).

It may also be suggested that the young boy is always extremely spoiled by his mother who sees in him the image of his father, and consequently allows him all sorts of liberties. The young daughter, by contrast, is trained to be submissive, retiring, and subservient to her "lord and master."[14] The result of this distribution of roles is, on the one hand, a rampant, grotesque Don Juan who begins his early training during adolescence and is admired for his conquests, and on the other, a maiden whose whole life and family honour revolve around the preservation of her virginity.[15]

An additional factor, worthy of note in this connection, is the anti-clerical syndrome which is intimately tied in with the home situation. The male adolescent, in the process of rebelling against his mother's domination, also rebels against her religious practices. But on a deeper level he has also rejected his father who has long since left home after brutalizing the mother. The father is subsequently replaced

[14] In recent years this has begun to change, especially in the large cities. Nevertheless, Mexico, as well as the rest of Latin America, is sorely in need of a strong Women's Liberation Movement.

[15] Segura Millán, p. 549.

by a new father-image, the priest, to whom the mother now turns for consolation. The son's rejection of the father is transferred to the priest. The father's hatred of the priest also increases as a result of the shift in allegiance. And thus the cycle continues, gathering momentum in apparently never-ending fashion.[16]

One does not have to accept wholeheartedly the psychoanalytical interpretation of the Mexican character. Yet it must be admitted that this approach has its attractive, and certainly intriguing, aspects—especially in light of attempted explanations of Mexican history. Thus, for example, the War of Independence represents the rebellion of the son against the father. The United States, which originally inspired Independence, gradually changed its image from that of the older brother to the possessive father, responsible for the loss of Mexican territory—symbolically represented by the castration of the son. Finally, the Revolution of 1910 may be viewed as a struggle against dictatorship; or in other words, against a powerful, arbitrary Gallicized father who would have nothing to do with a weak indigenous son.[17]

One could also point out that a perspective which attempts to give a picture of Mexican characterology in terms of sexual conflict tends to lean excessively upon historical factors—important though these may be. Current social aspects—at least in Ramírez' study—are not given their due consideration.

González Pineda takes a similar approach. Utilizing Freudian terminology, he attempts to interpret the Mexican psyche in terms of the interaction between the national ego and the superego. The national ego is, of course, equivalent to the collective ego of the inhabitants of Mexico—their emotional and instinctive needs which crave satisfaction. The collective superego represents the externally organized value system, the cultural norms and ideals. Superego structures are illustrated by the State and Church, which supposedly strive to approach these norms in day-to-day experience. As cultural organizations become more complex with the passage of time, fragmentation within the superego increases. The conflict between Church and State is a noteworthy example.

González Pineda finds that there have been serious defects in both the national ego and superego. An historical analysis of the clash between the European and the Indo-American cultures reveals the rather obvious fact that the imposition of the new socioeconomic organization met with a wide variety of responses, including different degrees of acceptance and rejection. Then, too, the political and religious structure of the superego never did function properly in its role of attempting to give the national ego the assurance it needed. For

---

[16] Francisco González Pineda, *El Mexicano: su dinámica psicosocial* (4th ed., Editorial Pax-Mexico, 1971), p. 80.
[17] Ramírez, pp. 71-72.

example, the Mexican—at first governed by a representative of the King—was forced after Independence to choose between a European power and the United States, as to which to be subservient to and attempt to emulate.[18] As for the Church, the other superego institution, its clergy had always failed to give the population the much-needed love and comfort. It had, instead, been severe and distant in its attitude, grotesque in its ritual, and characterized by continual conflict (pp. 102-103). The result was an insecure national ego, fragmented to begin with, because of the conflict of national identities. The schizoid ego was unable to establish proper contact, in psychoanalytical terms, with the object, i.e., with external reality. In this, as well as similar cases, the ego didn't like what it saw, and in order to evade its own reality, it visualized an idealization of that reality with which it then tried to identify. In the Mexican circumstance the national ego could not tolerate the totality of its external reality, and therefore tended to select only what it believed to be favourable aspects thereof, in order to satisfy its needs. That is why, for example, foreign constitutions were adopted as models. These were thought to be ideal; they would gratify the schizoid ego. They described what Mexicans would like to be, i.e., foreigners, not Mexicans, thus demonstrating in vivid fashion their alienation from reality (pp. 132-33). In short, the problem of multiple identities, characteristic of the national ego—creoles, mestizos, Indians—was complicated by a similar crisis of identity in the superego as well. The old superego (Spain) had been defeated. Now that Independence was a fact, the new father-image (in this case, France) was to serve as the guiding light. The only fly in the ointment was that the father whom the children now tried to imitate was totally different; so different, in fact, that he could not be imitated. The model was European, not Mexican. The new "ideal father" was not in accord with reality.

* * * * *

The war between Mexico and the United States can also be fitted into the psychoanalytical structure. The loss of Texas and California had its psychological significance. Mexico, in its adolescent stage, was able to rediscover positive aspects, inherited from Spain, as a result of the war against the "Colossus of the North." Now that a new enemy had appeared so close to its border—an enemy which had previously been admired—the Mexican was able to reconcile the antagonistic forces represented by the Spanish-Indian antinomy. In short, he could now transcend and shake off, as Carrión states, his "Oedipus complex which still throbbed in his psychological relation with Spain."[19]

[18] González Pineda, pp. 110-11.
[19] Carrión, p. 30. Thus turns out to be a strange statement in view of Carrión's earlier assertion to the effect that Spain represented the powerful, sadistic father during

In order to avenge the defeat caused by the "Trauma of 1847," and compensate for his own weakness, the Mexican could now take refuge in the world of wishful thinking and fantasy. He could either hope that some alien political power would humiliate the United States, or he could dream of violating three or four blond *gringas*, thanks to what he believed to be his superior virility, certainly more effective than that of the *gringos!* (pp. 33-34).

Conflict situations at both levels—the collective superego and the national ego—provide the necessary insight for an understanding of certain "undesirable" traits to be found in the Mexican. According to González Pineda, they have produced attitudes of suspicion, lack of trust, and aggressiveness.[20] The same author, in a subsequent publication, continues his diagnosis of negative characteristics via the presentation of a series of vignettes or case studies. The Mexican's destructive tendencies constitute the core of the study.[21] His aggressiveness and duplicity are weapons of both attack and defence. In each case we are dealing with techniques utilized to render more tolerable the internal as well as external reality of the individual ego.

Various phases of daily behaviour are characterized by acts of hostility. Although acts of aggression occur in other national groups, they are much more persistent and frequent in Mexico, where they also tend to become collective in nature (p. 91). Repressed egos have their roots in paranoid conceptions of reality. The love-hate relationship which the Mexican bears toward his mother engenders within him a feeling of guilt, a feeling which he cannot face up to, and consequently, he seeks a way out. His aggressions represent the escape valve. González Pineda presents five individual cases to illustrate his thesis: the inspector who accepts bribes, the driving habits of the average car owner, the corrupt newspaper reporter, the secret agent, and the professional killer.

One is tempted to question this apparently oversimplified explanation of individual neuroses which supposedly have their origins in history. Conversely, historical development is not to be explained solely in psychological terms. These may be important, but they do not constitute the exclusive frame of reference. Presenting individual case studies as representative of different segments of the population and pointing to these as examples of collective behaviour patterns is likewise open to criticism.[22]

the Conquest, as opposed to the masochistic, passive Indian earth in what was essentially an erotic love affair which ended in a violent and far from tender union (p. 23).

[20] González Pineda, p. 98.

[21] Francisco González Pineda, *El Mexicano: psicología de su destructividad* (6th ed., Editorial Pax-Mexico, 1972).

[22] The case of the automobile driver is indeed convincing. This writer can testify personally—after having lived in Mexico City for months on end—to countless infuriating experiences as a pedestrian. Crossing the street, even with the traffic light in one's favour, is an awesome adventure. The pedestrian is expected to *run* not walk across

Mexican aggressiveness, then, as a symptom of pride and arrogance—a cover-up for constant conflict with one's environment—erupts easily, given the proper stimuli. Violent aggression—the point bears repetition—is a form of escape from basic problems of insecurity. The Mexican wants to be feared. The male principle is opposed to such qualities as docility, reconciliation and dependency; these are considered feminine attributes.[23] Perhaps this would explain the fact, according to Segura Millán, that Mexico can boast of the highest criminal rate in the entire world.[24] Yet this same author tempers his harsh criticism by admitting that criminality is not to be explained solely in terms of psychology. One cannot ignore the demographic factor, economic inflation, and family dissolution. "We are violent because we are poor, and not because we are Mexicans" (p. 533). Yet other national groups, e.g., Chinese and Hindus, are also extremely poor; their delinquency rate is low.

Machismo can also manifest itself in other ways. For example, consideration for the sensibilities of one's neighbours is unheard of; noise will cease when one gets tired, not because one realizes suddenly that it may be offensive.

These neurotic symptoms, then, can be said to be the outgrowth of the conflict between conscious culture and the primitive unconscious. The mestizo oscillates between an emotional view of the universe and the scientific view of reality. However, this conflict between indigenous magical and Spanish logical constructs can also produce exceptionally positive results. In the field of art, for example, the Mexicans have found that this antinomy, far from creating obstacles, has yielded some of the finest works of their kind. Northrop's admiration for colonial architecture is, perhaps, referred to more often than that of other writers in this respect. "Fortunately," he writes, "the destruction of Indian values was not complete. Certain fragments of the native in-

the street, for fear of being struck down. The number of such incidents is sufficiently large as to make a generalization plausible. Yet one does well to hesitate. Mexico City exhibits all the unwelcome symptoms of a huge metropolis, true of other congested cities as well: rapid business expansion, population growth at a dizzying pace, and thorough-fares glutted with cars whose drivers are—many of them—seemingly unaware of such elementary concepts as courtesy on the road or the pedestrian's right of way. *Machismo* behind the wheel—as compensation for feelings of inadequacy—serves to bolster one's belief that he is acting in a world such as he would like it to be, rather than one which is the way it is. The only trouble is that it can and does produce catastrophic results.

The noted playwright, Rodolfo Usigli, adds his share of grist to the mill in this connection. He speaks of the "romantic need of the Mexican (chauffeur) to play continually with his own life as well as with those of others, in order to overcome his inferiority complex." Furthermore, he is incapable of the discipline and concentration so necessary to the performance of a job well done. It is this quality which "transforms the Mexican worker into a brilliant butterfly flitting about from one task to another in order to compensate for his inability to specialize in a single one." (Rodolfo Usigli, "Epílogo sobre la hipocresía del mexicano" [1938], in *El Gesticulador* [Mexico: Editorial Stylo, 1947], p. 175.)

[23] Paz, p. 26.
[24] Segura Millán, p. 531.

sight, especially in the aesthetic sphere, persisted. To these were added certain superior, more humane religious practices of worship and the ecclesiastical, architectural forms which Christian Spaniards brought."[25] Nor are the frescos by the famous trio[26] allowed to pass without comment. The Mexican appreciation of colour and form is analyzed in detailed fashion. It is not logically formulated theory, but rather "the passionately felt, aesthetic materials," that interest the Mexican.[27]

Perhaps one of the most striking manifestations of the Mexican's *machismo* is his scorn in the face of death. He can take a life or risk his own with the same degree of indifference as that displayed by the Aztec priests who sacrificed their victims for ceremonial purposes. Yet it has been asserted that this serenity of the *macho* is in reality a mask which hides the fear and insecurity caused by obstacles in the environment which appear to be insurmountable. Miserable socioeconomic conditions exert such pressure upon the lower-class Mexican that for him life has become cheap. Yet it costs a great deal to sustain it. On the other hand, death doesn't cost anything. To seek it is equivalent to taking refuge in the maternal womb where man can no longer be overtaken by suffering of any sort.[28] The same thought is expressed by Paz: "The Mexican's indifference in the face of death is sustained by his indifference to life ... to die is natural and even desirable; the sooner the better."[29] Life has cured the Mexican of fear, suggests Paz. Both life and death lack meaning. Yet despite this, the Mexican makes a cult of death. Death fascinates and seduces him, perhaps because it revenges him against life (p. 49). The Mexican oscillates between two extremes: "between intimacy and reserve, the cry and the silence, the fiesta and the wake ..." (p. 54). In the case of the fiesta, he has the opportunity to "open up," so to speak, to escape from himself and "leap over the wall of solitude" (p. 41) which confines him during the rest of the year. By means of a cathartic-like process, he frees himself from the established norms, only to emerge, subsequently, "purified and strengthened from this plunge into chaos" (p. 43). However, concludes Paz, in either case, whether it be the fiesta or the wake, the Mexican shuts himself off from the world, from both life and death (p. 54).

A related approach, utilized to explain Mexican weakness, is suggested by Segura Millán. In his formative period the Mexican felt

[25] F. S. C. Northrop, *The Meeting of East and West* (New York: Macmillan, 1946), p. 22.

[26] Rivera, Orozco, and Siqueiros.

[27] Northrop, p. 61.

[28] Carrión, pp. 19-20.

[29] Paz, p. 48. On All Souls' Day in early November, children eat candy in the shape of skulls and skeletons. Popular songs, with death as the principal theme, confirm the Mexican's scorn vis-à-vis its inevitable advent, for which he is always prepared. His joking about it—or any other misfortune—likewise amounts to a safety valve. (Salvador Reyes Nevárez, *El amor y la amistad an el mexicano* [Mexico: Porrúa y Obregón, 1952], pp. 70-71.)

alone and abandoned, situated between two worlds and not being at
home in either. Rejected by both cultures, he conjured up a third world
within which he achieved satisfactory status. This quixotic-like divorce
from reality made for an increased lack of responsibility. The Mexican,
unable to handle a situation, preferred to avoid it.[30] In short, a feeling
of constant dissatisfaction was far from conducive to a desire to see a
project through to a successful conclusion. A spirit of fatalism made
him unable or unwilling to improve his status quo. He always tended to
blame external conditions—never himself—for failure of any kind. Yet
in all fairness—if one speaks of cultural antecedents—it should be
remembered that the supposed lack of productivity which the Mexican
is accused of may conceivably have its origin in pre-Columbian times.
For let it not be forgotten that the indigenous ancestors managed a type
of economy which was designed to give immediate satisfaction. There
was no incentive to save for a "rainy day."

This lack of initiative has made the Mexican resort to family or
political "connections" for the purpose of rising in the socioeconomic
scale. Indolence and hard work do not go together. Hence, the complete submission to the father-image, especially in government circles,
which dispenses favours and rewards on a personal basis (p. 523).

It should also be remembered that the mystical concept of work—
an integral part of the indigenous religious culture—was replaced by
economic slavery under the auspices of the Spaniard. Small wonder,
therefore, that the Mexican's attitude toward the work ethos should be
less than enthusiastic.

One of the most obvious symptoms of the Mexican sense of
inferiority—and which the Revolution of 1910 sought to eliminate—is
the Mexican's boundless admiration for what is foreign and the deni-
gration of his own cultural values.[31] This has been labelled *Malinchismo*,
derived from *La Malinche* (Malinalli or Marina), the interpreter and
mistress of Hernán Cortés. Marina herself, purported to be of noble
blood, had been taken prisoner and forced to work as a domestic slave
as a result of the wars between the various indigenous groups. It was
probably natural for her to see in the Spaniard a possible avenger who
would bring about the downfall of those who had vanquished her own
people. Unfortunately, history was to deal with her in cruel fashion.
Not only was she abandoned by Cortés after having borne him a son,
but the Mexican people as a whole, because of the destruction wrought
by the Conquistadores, made her the national scapegoat and object of
collective hatred. *La Malinche* had formed an alliance with the
Spaniard; hence, *Malinchismo* smacks of betrayal of native values. As
stated, the Mexican Revolution was a direct reaction. *Malinchismo* was

[30] Segura Millán, p. 519.
[31] Ibid., pp. 520-21.

woven into the fabric of the ruling circles of the dictatorial regime of Porfirio Díaz.

* * * * *

The psychoanalytical approach advocated by Jorge Carrión in 1952 was abandoned by him about two decades later. A second edition of his work appeared in 1970, to be followed immediately by a third. This is of interest, because in the last two editions the author adds a new chapter entitled "An Essay of Self-Criticism." Carrión has undergone a change of heart and rejects the psychoanalytical perspective within which he had earlier placed the entire problem of the essence of Mexicanness. Such a perspective, he now admits, leads only to a highly subjective approach, and results in erroneous, irrational speculation.[32] Carrión apparently re-read Marx and concluded that the psychological method he had utilized was rooted in idealism. Instead, a more valid approach would base itself on social materialism. When one concentrates on the conscious, the unconscious, and the subconscious, applying Freudian techniques (which were meant for individual cases) to the study of society, then one tends to forget about the necessity for examining the Mexican as an entity subject to the laws of historical materialism, and as a product of the influence of conflicting class relations. In short, all the myths and magic, asserts Carrión, as these are expounded in the first edition, converted the Mexican into a passive object, a robot. Mythology moulded him. The perspective had to be inverted, or rather, turned right side up; the Mexican—as in the case of man in general—should be studied as an active subject or agent, in relation to his environment; in other words, as one who makes history (p. 114).

Yet one must utter a word of caution. From the standpoint of dialectical materialism—which Carrión seems to adhere to—man is not exclusively an active agent either. True, Carrión's about-face is a healthy reaction to a point of view which would make man a passive victim, buffeted by external forces, a leaf blown about in the wind. However, Carrión himself must admit that man is active not in an absolute, all-dominant sense, but rather in that he strives to control and modify these same forces which exert pressure upon him, and reduce the amount of buffeting to which he is subjected.

To speak of a collective consciousness as though it were a static substance is to forget that social groups undergo change, that they are not homogeneous entities, and that, finally, they do not merely reflect this consciousness but, instead, study and transform it. Continuing his self-criticism, Carrión states further that the original edition did not

[32] Carrión, p. 110.

clarify the extent to which *all* social classes of Mexico shared in the beliefs, myths, and even superstitions; nor for that matter was the point made clear that the social psychology of the lower classes was a reflection of the ideology of the dominant social group. Finally, it is erroneous, confesses Carrión, to identify social repression with psychoanalytic repression. The latter is a phenomenon applied only to individuals (p. 120). The point seems well taken: a neurotic individual may try to return to the warmth and comfort of his mother's womb. On the other hand, an entire social class—if it is the victim of oppression—does not attempt to regress to an earlier stage of evolution. As a matter of fact, this may be precisely what the dominant class, the oppressor, would like it to do. However, Carrión's work, in its first edition, should not be discounted. What is, indeed, valid is the description of social phenomena, and the attempts made to understand them.

Still Carrión's subsequent assertion to the effect that the psychology of the lower classes is a reflection of the ideology of the ruling class may be disputed. Even Marxists admit that psychological drives and motivations may be locked in mortal combat with one another. The conflict between the "haves" and the "have-nots" is an obvious case in point. The "haves" may wish to impose their behaviour patterns as models to be followed. The "have-nots" may have other ideas on the subject. In fact, the self-same "have-nots" may change their psychology when they become "haves."

* * * * *

Anxiety, under normal circumstances, is a feeling which results from a temporary failure to solve a problem. Once a solution is arrived at, the anxiety tends to diminish or disappear altogether. However, since the Mexican feels he can never arrive at satisfactory solutions, his anxiety is constant, his frustrations multiply, and he continues to postpone attempts to attack the problem. This attitude may be said to find its reflection, interestingly enough, in some of the most frequently used, characteristically Mexican patterns of speech, as these refer to the concept of time. An outstanding example is the constant use of the term *ahorita* (the diminutive of *ahora*), which acquires a number of varied meanings, depending on mood and circumstance, e.g., "just a moment ago," "in a little while," "immediately." One may experience an exasperating delay of several hours, if not days or weeks, waiting for *ahorita* to be realized. Failing to comply with the expectations involved, the Mexican's frustration seeks a safety valve, and finds it—in the face of repeated failures—in the form of postponement or even deception (*ahorita*). Telling a lie is simply a method of covering up fear and insecurity.[33]

[33] Segura Millán, pp. 529-30.

Ahorita, perhaps the most commonly used expression in Mexican Spanish, provides insight into the phenomenological axis of the Mexican sense of time. The constant adding of suffixes to *ahorita*, to make the concept even more diminutive (e.g., *ahoritita, ahorititita*) is analogous to a constellation of concentric circles which represent the present. To grasp the essence of what is involved, one must travel in an *inward* direction, beginning with the outermost circle. The inner circle is "more present" than the outer. In short, we begin with *ahora* which is abstract and universal, and progress toward the centre of the smallest circle. Hence, *ahora, ahorita, ahoritita, ahorititita*,[34] in order to specify a more precise situation by reducing the span of time. Further reduction is achieved by dropping the first letter: *horita, horitita*, etc. Perhaps this diminution of the temporal element *ad infinitum* is an attempt to reduce to the tiniest particle possible the object or situation in question. Eventually, extending this process, theoretically at least, to the nth degree, makes one arrive at nothing! Space (the situation) is thus annihilated together with time. As though wishing to escape from the world (and himself), the Mexican reduces everything to nothingness and curls up within it (p. 139). The Mexican is the only Spanish-speaking individual who has operated in this way on the word *ahora*. *Ahorita* is his way of saying "yes," but not "when," or of saying "when" indefinitely, but not saying "yes" (p. 141)—an interesting and stimulating hypothesis at best, but one which still borders on speculation.

Another possible interpretation in this connection brings us back to *machismo*. The *macho* wishes to reduce to nothing the limited world within which he moves, and to belittle or ignore the pressure of time. By reducing to the utmost possible limits the concept of *ahora*, he shows that he is above it all. We are thus faced by an oscillation between two extremes: the individual who, figuratively speaking, curls up in a fetal position, and his opposite who bristles with raw, unfettered masculinity (p. 148).

Rounding out the picture is the Mexican's scorn of death, already referred to, his feeling that he has no history; he is therefore "inferior" or "inadequate," leading a meaningless existence, one completely annihilated by the use of *ahorita* (p. 150).[35]

---

[34] Isaías Altamirano, "El sentido mexicano del tiempo," *Filosofía y letras* 21, no. 41-42 (January-June 1951), 136-37.

[35] The Latin American in general, and the Mexican in particular, are supposedly indifferent to the passage of time. Rationalization has it that time "flows" through the individual, "possessing" him as it were, thereby converting him into a passive object and enabling him to merely enjoy its passing. In contrast, according to the popular stereotype, the "active," "voluntaristic" *gringo* takes possession of time, utilizes it, and converts it into material value ("time is money").

Since the Mexican is not a "slave" to time, he need not be so compulsive about being punctual, for example, in the matter of social commitments. The present writer has, on a number of occasions, had to wait from one to two hours beyond the time set for a given appointment.

Segura Millán seems quite harsh with respect to his countrymen. Not only does he find them lazy; they are also dishonest, disorganized, and disorderly.[36] The Mexican's perennial conflict with his environment, and the frustration which ensues, would also account—at least in part—for the high rate of criminality (p. 531). Mexican pride breeds suspicion—hardly a sound basis for the formation of a lasting friendship. Mexicans tend to isolate themselves; there is a marked absence of sociability. The Mexican is friendly only in the presence of foreigners; in the presence of his countrymen, aggressiveness takes over (p. 556).

These generalizations are certainly open to criticism. Segura Millán and others who have indulged in similar judgments can be faulted for not having produced any statistical data to substantiate their claims. A case in point: Is the political element in the social structure, e.g., the "cult of personality" (the local "boss," the community leader, or the government functionary), determined by *machismo*? Is this the all-powerful factor which conditions social relations? Or is it perhaps the other way round? Do social relations give additional weight to *machismo*? Perhaps there is reciprocal interaction and the two elements reinforce each other. Psychology certainly influences human behaviour, but is this the exclusive determinant in the picture? The answer seems obvious.

Contradicting Segura Millán's assertion that Mexicans are not friendly is an equally subjective claim to the effect that friendship is one of the human relationships which is cultivated most effectively in Mexico.[37] A friend is deemed worthy and deserving of any and all sacrifices. One is considered an ingrate if he does not offer all he possesses to aid a friend in need. Friendship is characterized by a sense of refinement, "one of our most outstanding characteristics" (p. 15). This is certainly a powerful factor, which aids in the perpetuation of humanism, a quality which seems to be on the decline in other countries (p. 93).

The subjective element is clearly evident in these two judgments which contradict each other so sharply. Perhaps, as though to offset this extreme subjectivity, one of the first attempts made to introduce some measure of objectivity was undertaken by Gómez Robleda.[38] This involved a diagnostic questionnaire, designed to arrive at a composite picture of various components of psychological maladjustment, as evinced by middle-class Mexicans. By means of test items, e.g., presenting word lists as stimuli, representative of different categories of

This attitude can also be romanticized and made to look highly attractive. This writer noticed the following sign, posted in a restaurant in Guanajuato: "A good holiday is one spent among people whose notions of time are vaguer than yours."

[36] Segura Millán, p. 525.

[37] Reyes Nevárez, pp. 73-74.

[38] José Gómez Robleda, *Psicología del mexicano* (Mexico: Universidad Nacional Autónoma de México, 1962).

centres of interest, the author hoped to evoke reactions which would yield a constellation of psychological patterns, chiefly negative in nature, for the group tested. The words were selected for their ability to cause annoyance which was subsequently measured in terms of the type and frequency of the reaction evinced. Approximately five hundred subjects were tested in this experiment; all ages were represented, beginning with adolescents and ending with middle-aged men and women, about evenly divided. The centres of interest involved such items as family and school relationships, work in rural areas and urban settings, illness, guilt feelings, economic conditions, and finally, attitudes toward the unknown or mysterious. The great majority of the people tested consisted of middle-class professionals, living in the capital; more than fifty per cent were students. Conspicuously absent were members of the working and peasant classes. The author himself admits that in view of the findings, it is inappropriate to speak of *the* psychology of the Mexican. There are undoubtedly variations to be found as one proceeds from one social class to another.

Among the interesting conclusions to emerge from this experiment is the fact that guilt feelings seem to increase with age. Similarly, there is an increase in disturbances associated with the unknown and unforeseeable, more so in men than in women. The techniques of this pioneering venture may well be extended to other socioeconomic groups. As things stand, it is a contribution to the psychology of the middle-class Mexican. Yet as Gómez Robleda himself points out, it is difficult to know, judging from the results, whether the psychological aspects revealed are more middle class than Mexican or vice versa (p. 54).

Samuel Ramos himself admitted in his pioneer study of Mexican characterology that he had not had available any antecedents to guide him. He was clearly dissatisfied with his work, and urged others to continue the exploration of the Mexican psyche. The gloomy picture which he had painted in his *Profile* . . . stimulated him to delve further into the facets he had described, and to discover values he hadn't seen before. Almost two decades following his dissection of the Mexican character, he asked himself whether the traits described could be applied equally to both Indians and whites. The differences between the two groups, he concluded, were not as profound as appeared to be the case. The mestizos and creoles had many characteristics in common with the Indians.[39] Although there were different regional groupings, the impact of cultural forces—especially the Revolution of 1910—brought these closer together and moulded their collective consciousness. Historical events, all of them negative—e.g., anarchy, dictatorship, the War of 1847, French intervention, the Díaz regime, un-

[39] Samuel Ramos, "En torno a las ideas sobre el mexicano," *Cuadernos Americanos* 57, no. 3 (May-June 1951), 105.

favourable publicity abroad—had resulted in self-denigration and "devaluation" by the Mexican himself, with the resultant loss of self-confidence and group solidarity. Psychologically, this negative national image was thrust below the level of the individual's consciousness; as a result, he resorted to compensatory mechanisms. Illusory ideas which he adopted caused him to conceal and falsify his own reality. He adopted foreign models of behaviour because they seemed to have worked well abroad; hence, they would, he assumed, function efficiently at home as well (pp. 107-108).

The status of one's nation, claimed Ramos, is bound to affect individual behaviour. For example, a citizen of a powerful nation acts with assurance both within and beyond its borders. If this sense of collective well-being is deficient, he will utilize all sorts of compensatory devices. In the absence of a healthy balance between group feeling and individual conduct, the Mexican exhibits aggression, resentment, deception, arrogance—all of which are masks for timidity and lack of confidence (p. 109). Solitude, too, is a symptom of this condition. Ramos disagreed with Paz who had maintained that solitude was the end product of a voluntary decision. On the contrary, maintained Ramos, it was a refuge sought out by the Mexican due to his anti-social nature, a consequence of his timidity, distrust, and hypersensitivity. The love of solitude is enjoyed to the full when it is a privilege limited to those possessed of a rich inner life, "an aristocracy of spirit," such as that of poets, philosophers, or mystics; "it is not an attribute of the common man" (p. 110).

Ramos' work inevitably provoked critical commentary. Emilio Uranga was one of the first to challenge his basic thesis of inferiority. Writing in the same issue,[40] he emphasized the distinction between "inferiority" and "inadequacy"—a point he had made earlier in an article dealing with the philosophy of the Mexican character.[41]

Inferiority, claims Uranga, is one of the modalities of inadequacy, but not the only one (p. 136). Ramos, according to Uranga, asserts that inferiority serves to explain the Mexican's character. But what is the nature of this character? Adopting an existentialist position, Uranga presents the Mexican in terms of a constellation of factors which include a generous dose of emotionalism and inactivity, plus a never-ending tendency to brood over one's experiences. The Mexican adopts techniques of protection to guard himself against the shocks to what he considers his inner fragility. This is illustrated by his attempts at unobtrusiveness, often bordering on concealment and hypocrisy, which are merely symptoms of his incurable fragility. He constantly feels threatened and subject to destruction; he is afraid of being over-

[40] "Notas para un estudio del mexicano," in ibid., p. 114.
[41] Emilio Uranga, "Ensayo de una ontología del mexicano," *Cuadernos Americanos* 54, no. 2 (March-April, 1949), 135-48.

whelmed by a sense of "nothingness," of ceasing to exist. Obstacles in the way of fulfilment of his tasks do not appear as a challenge to be overcome. Instead, they cause him to withdraw even further into himself. He is reluctant to make decisions, preferring to postpone the decision-making process indefinitely. This lack of will to act expresses itself even in the most ordinary day-to-day chores, such as not answering the telephone for fear of the responsibility it might entail.[42] It is this sense of evasion, Uranga maintains, that is derived from a feeling of insufficiency or inability to cope with a situation. Inadequacy is a result of an imagined sense of inferiority, and eventually becomes transformed into inferiority itself (p. 139).

Inactivity, if not outright paralysis of action, in the face of obstacles, leads to angry protest because things aren't going just right. To this configuration is now added the concept of dignity, which converts inactivity into a virtue. Dignity in this sense (inherited, perhaps, from the Spanish *hidalgo?*) is expressed as reluctance to soil oneself, i.e., become involved in tasks considered to be beneath one's social status. Dignity, disinclination to perform, and inner fragility are thus linked together.[43]

A sense of melancholy is the result of frustrated experiences. The individual resorts to re-living memories. He reflects on the precarious structure of his state of being, often fleeing from reality and taking refuge in dreams and fantasies.

The Mexican, ontologically, oscillates between being and non-being. He lives in a state of constant anxiety, uncertain as to what the next moment has in store for him. Existing within the shadowy zone of the "accident," he never knows what to rely on; his existence is precarious, far from solid or substantial, and therefore, "insufficient." But— and this is Uranga's central thesis—"insufficiency of accidence" is not the same as inferiority.[44] To be inferior, claims Uranga, is an ideal for

---

[42] A personal note: One becomes accustomed, for example, to the oft-repeated litany: "The maid failed to tell me that you had called." Or else: "I did get the message and called you back, but you were out" (which turns out to be untrue, since I had been sitting for hours, glued to the phone!). All of this, merely to avoid coming to grips with a situation, even on a most elementary plane.

[43] Reyes Nevárez speaks of the quality of dignity as a national virtue. It is associated with a certain elegant haughtiness for which an audience is a necessary prerequisite so that the individual may show his complete indifference in the face of a task he considers unworthy. In too many cases, this posture is a pretext for not doing what has to be done. (Salvador Reyes Nevárez, pp. 37-38.)

[44] "Ensayo de una ontología del mexicano," p. 145. Leopoldo Zea also offers a critical observation in this connection, one which is certain to enrage Latin Americans. Commenting upon the well-known syndrome involving the widespread use of university titles (although not restricted to Mexico), he ventures the suggestion that the excessive use in ordinary conversation of "Doctor," "Licenciado," "Ingeniero," "Arquitecto," etc., may at times be viewed as a form of ostentation—conceivably a mechanism to disguise a feeling of insecurity. (*La esencia de lo americano* [Buenos Aires: Editorial Pleamar, 1971]), p. 80.

many Mexicans.[45] A sense of inferiority resolves many problems for them. It is their life norm. Furthermore, an "inferior" situation is not necessarily "inadequate," nor is the converse true. For example, a meal may be inadequate, but not inferior. There are "superior" meals which are insufficient, as well as "adequate" diets which are inferior in quality.[46] In short, the concept of adequacy involves meeting to a satisfactory degree the needs of a given level of existence, whereas the idea of superiority expresses a higher stage in the hierarchy of levels. Applied to the Mexican scene, cultural activity may or may not satisfy the needs of a given status within clearly defined limits. If such satisfaction is not forthcoming, then the culture may be said to be inadequate. Adequacy or inadequacy of Mexican culture is measured on a scale of "intrinsic" evaluation, i.e., without reference to other cultures. However, if such comparison is brought into the picture, then the consequent "extrinsic" evaluation dictates the use of such terms as "superior" and "inferior," and even in that case it would be difficult, if not invalid, to speak of an "inferior" culture. Thus, if Mexicans were to view themselves through European eyes, the terms "superior" and "inferior" might conceivably crop up. However, Uranga sees no reason for this. Mexicans do not have to accept judgments emanating from abroad. Uranga admits that whether or not Mexican culture is "adequate," the fact remains that the Mexican *thinks* his culture is "inferior" to that of Europe. Nevertheless, this attitude should not imply the existence of an actual inferiority complex, as Ramos indicated in his pioneer study. Acknowledging the existence of a hierarchy of values is not equivalent to manifesting an inferiority complex. Far from indicating inferiority, it may well point to the recognition of one's "inadequacy," together with a corresponding desire to remedy the condition (pp. 52-53).

Finally, it should be pointed out that admiration of other "superior" values may lead to an attitude of defeatism. This is a deplorable situation, since such resignation and impotence serve to blunt one's desire to utilize these values. He who does not *feel* "inferior" strives to appropriate and adapt so-called "superior" values to his circumstances. The real inferiority complex makes its appearance only when the "superior" level is looked up to and cannot be attained. At that point is is the object of envy and compensated for by an imagined superiority. But then this phenomenon is no longer a specifically "Mexican" trait, but rather a characteristic that can be found in other national and ethnic groups.

[45] "Notas para un estudio del mexicano," *Cuadernos Americanos* 57, no. 3 (May-June 1951), 121.

[46] Emilio Uranga, *Análisis del ser del mexicano* (Mexico: Porrúa y Obregón, 1952), p. 51.

CHAPTER TWO

THE
SOCIOLOGICAL APPROACH

Sociologists, too, have seen in Mexico a rich mine of possibilities for the purpose of undertaking studies of national character. Early attempts, during the first two decades of the present century, reveal a relatively unsophisticated approach to complex problems.[1] Techniques are refined and improved as time goes on, research centres are established,[2] and native as well as foreign sociologists contribute voluminously to an increasingly large number of publications.[3]

A pioneer work in Mexican sociology[4] discusses three classes of women, a subject of particular interest in view of the developing Women's Liberation Movement. According to Gamio, the servant class (*la mujer sierva*) exists only for work, maternity, and if time permits, pleasure. All three factors, in that order, constitute a "zoological action," imposed by circumstances and the environment. The second group is labelled the "feminist" woman, for whom pleasure is more of a sport. Maternity for this type is not a basic or important function, since the "feminist"—more likely to be found in large cities—tends to be "masculine" in her behaviour. Finally, the "feminine" woman—the ideal for Gamio—avoids both extremes; she is situated between the two types referred to above (pp. 211-12). Pointing to the degree of illiteracy and lack of educational opportunities that existed in his day, Gamio concluded that, according to European standards, there were proportionately fewer representatives of the first two categories, and more of the third, than should have been the case sociologically (p. 222). Of course, this conclusion was based on the hypothesis that the greater the illiteracy, the larger the number of servant women.

Another attempted correlation was made with reference to the ability to work. One perceives a considerable degree of speculation in

[1] For example, Manuel Gamio, *Forjando patria* (Mexico: Librería de Porrúa Hermanos, 1916).

[2] Such as those connected with the *Universidad Nacional Autónoma de México*, and the *Colegio de México*.

[3] Perhaps the most popular works to appear in English have been written by the highly controversial sociologist Oscar Lewis—controversial from the Mexican point of view.

[4] Gamio (see footnote 1 of this chapter).

the treatment of this aspect of the study. For example, the population is divided into two groups: (1) the indigenous and "heavily" mestizo; and (2) the European and "lightly" mestizo. The first group, it is asserted, is sluggish in its work habits, but more resistant and able to stand up under adverse conditions. On the other hand, the workers in the second category can generate more energy than those in group one, within a given time interval. Their muscular development is apparently superior, and their nutrition better (pp. 249-50). The conclusion seems rather obvious: variations in the ability to work depend upon geographic and climatic conditions, as well as the economic circumstances in effect. Less acceptable is the generalization concerning this ability with reference to biologically acquired characteristics, e.g., the distinction made between "lighter" and "darker" or "more heavily" mestizo.

Gamio recommended that more research be performed with respect to the Mexican's working habits in order to determine his normal labour capacity. Unfortunately, the term "normal" was never defined. Yet work habits are not discussed in isolation by this author. They are linked with the Mexican's personality traits. A comparison is made with the powerful neighbour to the north, as a result of which the Mexican comes out second-best. In the United States, maintained Gamio, the dollar is the Almighty. All else seems forgotten. However, once the American comes into possession of his riches, a respectable portion of that income is expended to promote cultural activities for the welfare of his fellow-citizens. Rockefeller has extorted millions upon millions of dollars from the people; on the other hand, he has spent fifty or a hundred million in order to build a scientific research centre.[5]

By contrast—and this is the essential point—Mexicans who accumulate their wealth spend it all on items of luxury. The more they earn, the more grasping and greedy they become. Only one in a thousand will contribute to any sort of effort for the common good. "When have our financial tycoons ever established schools, research institutes, artistic academies, in *disinterested* fashion . . . ? Never!" (p. 270). We always accuse the Americans of being utilitarians and crass materialists, concludes Gamio. We, Mexicans, are far worse than they are.

Much has happened on both sides of the Río Grande since the above was written. Yet it is refreshing to note—the activities of North American financial operations in Latin America notwithstanding—that this Mexican scholar, more than a half century ago, had the courage to say in print that there were also humanistic endeavours being carried on in the United States. In too many cases, Latin American intellectuals have claimed a monopoly on humanism—a psychological device in the form of a compensatory mechanism, utilized as a weapon in their opposition to a rampant capitalism.

[5] Ibid., p. 269.

* * * * *

Psychology and sociology seem to join hands in agreeing that it is difficult if not invalid to speak of a Mexican "type." The ground seems safer if one's analysis is restricted to a given social group, e.g., middle class, urban proletariat, peasant woman, student, etc., although, admittedly, there are variations within each of these categories. Nevertheless, in spite of these possible pitfalls, María Elvira Bermúdez undertakes a study and dissection of Mexican family life, touching upon first-hand observation in the province of Durango, as well as in the Federal District of the capital, supplemented by research data taken from other areas. Bermúdez had hoped, in this way, to obtain a composite picture from a geographical point of view. The Federal District was considered a good cross section of the population.

As for relationships between the sexes, Bermúdez does not make any distinction between members of, for example, the middle class and the peasant group. One wonders whether *all* men and women behave in the same way, regardless of social class. Witness, for example, such statements as: fidelity in the male is unheard of; this is considered an insult to his masculinity, whereas fidelity in the female is axiomatic. After the husband abandons his wife, she cannot belong to anyone else. His *machismo* leads him to affirm: "She is either mine or nobody's."[6] Nor does the man who replaces the husband represent a stable relationship. He may even be despised by the woman during their more intimate moments, since she knows that eventually she will be discarded, or else he will be replaced by still another man who can offer her more in a material sense. Material standards thus acquire a greater importance than moral and intellectual values. The woman's attitude is one of passive resignation. She is willing to put up with her lot for reasons of security (p. 58). At times, her submission to the male is exaggerated. This accentuation of so-called "feminine" characteristics is dubbed *hembrismo*, the female counterpart of *machismo* (p. 93). Under these circumstances women can never be friends; they must always be rivals in the struggle for subsistence. As a common saying has it: "Just let my husband give me the cash; he can save his kisses for the other."[7]

The Mexican is not the only man in the universe who is convinced that he is superior to woman. But he is constantly concerned about this, and in exaggerated fashion. Love for him is synonymous with passion; he is obsessed by woman even though he despises her. His vanity convinces him that she must ever remain faithful to him, even after he leaves her. His interest in her is purely physical; he cannot take "no" for an answer. A woman who disdains him is a traitor and an affront to his

---

[6] María Elvira Bermúdez, *La vida familiar del mexicano* (Mexico: Porrúa y Obregón, 1955), p. 52.

[7] "Que mi marido me dé a mí los pesos, y a otra los besos" (p. 60).

machismo. Such action on her part is inconceivable, since he is blind to his own defects and limitations (pp. 85-88).

The outstanding weakness of Bermúdez' study is its complete absence of controlled experimentation, a fact which stands out in analyses by others, as well. Speculation and generalization, no matter how attractive, are no substitute for vigorous, scientific procedures. Yet Bermúdez' intentions are laudable. The Mexican's circumstances have generated a series of characteristics which, on the surface at least, seem peculiar to him alone. It is not a question of being better or worse than anyone else. It is, rather, one which involves the determination of certain factors so that tomorrow's Mexican may be better than the present-day variety.

Can *machismo* and *hembrismo*, for example, be modified for the better? Both are the result of group influences. Man's nature can be changed by the conditions of his social environment, maintains Bermúdez. This has always been an optimistic premise, the validity of which has not been demonstrated in more than two thousand years. Nevertheless, Bermúdez has faith. There is a difference, she claims, between character and temperament. Temperament refers to one's manner of reacting to his environment; it is biologically unchangeable, whereas character is formed as a result of personal experiences and is modifiable to a point, depending upon knowledge of oneself. Assuming that this is a valid distinction (although one may question it), it follows that two people of similar temperament may differ in character. Hence, according to Bermúdez, the Mexican's temperament, in spite of its sensuality, is not an obstacle in the path of his character formation. There is hope for improvement. How? By destroying the prejudices which result in *machismo* and *hembrismo*. By replacing foolhardiness with authentic valour, and feminine abnegation with a desire for dignity. Sexual harmony is indeed possible! (pp. 122-23). One can only applaud the faith in progress in this area. There have been isolated signs in this direction, but the wheels grind ever so slowly. Of late, more deference has been shown to women by men, and among limited segments of Mexican youth there has even been some encouraging opposition to *machismo*. But the road continues to be long and hard.

* * * * *

In contrast to Bermúdez, whose study concentrates on the capital district, Fromm and Maccoby have provided us with a view in depth of the socioeconomic and cultural patterns of a peasant community in the state of Morelos.[8] Their study is an attempt to test the theory of social

[8] Erich Fromm and Michael Maccoby, *Social Character in a Mexican Village* (Englewood Cliffs, N.J.: Prentice-Hall, 1970).

character; i.e., character structure common to most members of a given group or class. It is based on the hypothesis that "a syndrome of character traits develops as an adaptation to the economic, social, and cultural conditions common to that group" (p. 16). Members of the group are motivated by their social character in such a way as to carry out their social and economic functions in optimum fashion. It follows that different classes do not have the same social character; the latter depends upon the role in the social structure. The characteristics which are described are, therefore, restricted to the villagers interviewed and cannot be applied to the "Mexican" in general. For example, there is a significant correlation between *machismo* and alcoholism. The alcoholic's *machismo* is merely a façade. Seventy-five percent of those interviewed were judged to be dominated by their wives. *Machismo* for the alcoholic is a reaction to his fear of women, a compensation for his feeling of weakness and passivity (p. 166). From the woman's point of view, Fromm and Maccoby affirm that many wives humour their husbands who parade their *machismo* in order to be able to function effectively. For the woman, *machismo* is an expression of immaturity. Even though the *macho* may dominate in the early years, the woman eventually takes command as the husband grows older (pp. 151-52). One noted American sociologist[9] has stated that *machismo* seems much weaker among the lower classes than in the middle and upper income groups (p. 17). Yet one must note from the title of this work that the sampling is not too representative. Lest an erroneous impression be created, there are also Mexican villagers who are productive and interested in the welfare of their families.[10]

Still another aspect of Mexican characterology is presented by Cantinflas, Mexico's most famous screen comic. Here we are faced with a caricature—the humourous and grotesque aspects of art—as a medium with which to illustrate the "essence" of the Mexican personality. Cantinflas represents the lowest rung in the socioeconomic ladder, the hobo. He is weak, malnourished, sad; he lives off leftovers found in garbage cans. Since he has no ambition whatsoever to improve his status, he cannot be said to suffer from an inferiority complex. Perhaps he is too far gone, since he prefers to hide in the anonymity of the slums.

Yet he is cunning. He avoids commitments. He neither affirms nor denies, continually oscillating between the two poles. In the presence of women or the police—representatives of love and death, respectively—he acts timidly. A slip of the tongue may compromise him, and he may end up either married or in jail.[11] The Mexican public

[9] Oscar Lewis, *Five Families* (New York: Science Editions, 1962), p. 17.

[10] Michael Maccoby, "Love and Authority: A Study of Mexican Villagers," *The Atlantic* 213, no. 3 (1964), 121-26.

[11] César Garizurieta, *Isagoge sobre lo mexicano* (Mexico: Porrúa y Obregón, 1952), pp. 54-55.

sees itself reflected in Cantinflas. The latter does not wish to appear stupid or too intelligent, and is always on the defensive in a hostile environment. Astuteness has replaced strength. Perhaps this explains his immense popularity.

Surprisingly, he also fights against social injustice; not consciously, to be sure, yet social conditions are always the target of his criticism. Since he never works on a permanent basis, he can hardly be said to belong to the proletariat or petite bourgeoisie. He scoffs at social norms. Like the *pícaro*, he uses mockery, farce, and irony as both an offensive and defensive weapon. Essentially, he is a "frustrated romantic" (p. 57).

Garizurieta claims that Cantinflas is most representative of Mexican style, particularly as this refers to his manner of thinking and feeling, and his attitude toward life (pp. 58-59). Yet is it not dangerous to generalize in this way on the basis of a prototype? Garizurieta, himself, admits that one must be extremely careful when speaking of "Mexican style," since no one has yet effected a valid structure of Mexican "spirit" or personality. The diversity of types makes it quite unlikely that these will some day jell into a stable, uniform modality. Mexican society is in a state of constant flux, due to its social and economic struggles. Such a dynamic condition runs counter to the possibility of arriving at a static Mexican "type." Nevertheless, this same author, like so many others, maintains that the individual Mexican suffers from a feeling of inferiority and insecurity. As in the case of Cantinflas, his actions are always characterized by uncertainty; he never takes a stand, preferring instead to hide behind the mask of anonymity. "He does not try to be his authentic self, but seeks rather to become depersonalized and to dissolve into a 'we' . . ." (p. 59). Yet in the next breath Garizurieta appears to contradict himself. The Mexican does not suffer from an inferiority complex (p. 60).[12] It is at this point that the North American makes an unexpected appearance for illustrative purposes. Garizurieta contrasts him with the Mexican. The former, it is stated, is a victim of this complex, since he has to compensate continually by affirming that his country is bigger and better than all the others. The Mexican, on the other hand, is not faced with this problem. He is aware of his shortcomings. He makes no secret of the fact that his world is small and limited, and has no desire to make his world bigger and more powerful, as is the case with his northern neighbour. One might add at this point that despite Garizurieta's assertions, the Mexican's feeling of inferiority does not seem to operate vis-à-vis his *southern* neighbours.

* * * * *

[12] Garizurieta does not distinguish clearly between "feeling" and "complex," although he does say that "complex" belongs to the world of the subconscious. By implication, "feeling" is conscious.

José Iturriaga is another sociologist who attempts to take inventory of so-called Mexican traits. He is aware of the fact that there are obstacles—philosophical and sociological—that stand in the way of a "characterology." From a philosophical point of view, two basic perspectives have always stood in opposition to each other: the rationalist and the historicist. The first has always spoken in terms of "universal" qualities of man; man has been and remains the same throughout the entire globe, regardless of his origin. This view has been contested by the assertion that man is conditioned by his circumstance, and his personality moulded accordingly, thus rendering him distinct from other personalities.

Iturriaga tends to lean toward the circumstantial approach. Each people has its own peculiar stamp, its set of collective reactions to its environment, i.e., its geographic, historical, social, and political circumstances. Nevertheless, in the case of Mexico, there are complicating factors which prevent one from formulating the "essence" of Mexican character, factors which introduce too many variables. For example, the very complexity of Mexico's past is a formidable impediment. One must consider the multiplicity of indigenous groups inhabiting the country prior to the Conquest, the *mestizaje* quality of the Spanish conquistador himself, and finally, the fact that cultural *mestizaje* is still in a process of fermentation.

Admittedly, the characteristics of the Mexican differ according to his geographical location, which is only one of several variables. Iturriaga, therefore, prefers to study the inhabitants of the central part of the country, where, he believes, *mestizaje* is most pronounced and firmly rooted. Since characterology is an attempt to describe the collective national subconscious, Iturriaga believes that a study which concentrates on the "lower middle" and "popular" classes, located in that region, is representative of the so-called Mexican "type."[13] It has to be assumed that by "popular," he means the lower class, both urban and rural, as well as the impoverished segments of the lower middle class, although, as a contemporary critic points out, "it is difficult from a conceptual point of view to establish the differences between 'popular classes' and 'poor middle classes.' . . ."[14]

Iturriaga's inventory of Mexican traits duplicates, in many instances, what has already been said by Ramos, Paz, and others. The low esteem in which the Mexican holds himself is a vestige of the colonial past, a characteristic of a conquered race. Inferiority and timidity produce their compensatory mechanisms, such as antisocial aspects of superiority, fearlessness in the face of death, and a sense of humour

[13] José E. Iturriaga, *La estructura social y cultural de México* (Mexico: Fondo de Cultura Económica, 1951), pp. 227-30.
[14] Raúl Béjar Navarro, *El mito del mexicano* (2nd ed., Mexico: Editorial Orientación, 1971), p. 168.

used as a weapon for both offensive and defensive purposes (of which Cantinflas is the archetype). Contrasts in behaviour are striking: violence versus delicacy and tenderness;[15] cockfights versus extremely artistic arrangements of floral decorations.[16]

However, the Mexican *mestizo*, as is to be expected, carries within himself not only the echoes of his Indian heritage; his individualism which results in a marked lack of cooperative spirit can be traced to the Spanish component of the cultural configuration. The individualistic spirit makes for a considerable degree of marginality in the sphere of political activity. Iturriaga compares the Mexican in this respect with the inhabitant of the United States, and finds that the social sense is more strongly developed in the latter. Quoting Daniel Cosío Villegas,[17] he states: "The strong point of the United States is its sense of collectivity, rather than the individual; Mexico's best element is the individual person, not the social factor."[18]

One may take issue with this snap judgment, especially when it is remembered that American individualism has always been contrasted with the collectivism of socialist countries. True enough, "rugged" individualism may have been modified, and programs of social concern increased. It is difficult, however, to demonstrate in convincing fashion the validity of such generalizations. It would, perhaps, be more accurate to speak of the American's sense of individualism in some areas, and his spirit of "teamwork" in others.

Iturriaga continues his comparison of the people living on either side of the Río Grande. When travelling abroad, for example, the Mexican gives a much better impression than the American (p. 234), a judgment which is highly questionable. Even if this were the case, the reason for such "typical" behaviour should not be too difficult to fathom. Usually, it is only the upper-class Mexican, possessed of all the usual social refinements, who has the wherewithal to travel. The "ugly" American who travels is representative of vast numbers of middle-class, and more recently, even of working-class, people who, perhaps, have not yet assimilated upper-class patterns of social behaviour. Iturriaga's comparison seems not only unsound, but gratuitous as well.

The Mexican's basic antagonism to politics and distrust of governmental machinery—the result of his opposition to enterprises of a social character—is compensated by his ability to form loyal and lasting friendships. Devotion to a person is valued more highly than loyalty to

[15] Iturriaga, p. 233.
[16] The highly inventive patterns formed by the numerous articles for sale to be found on the sidewalks of Mexico City constitute another example, not to mention the riot of colour and ingenious fireworks characteristic of the week-long celebration of Christmas in the Alameda and the Zócalo.
[17] Daniel Cosío Villegas, *Extremos de América* (Mexico: Fondo de Cultura Económica, 1949).
[18] Iturriaga, p. 234.

an idea. This is not peculiar to Mexico. The "cult of personality" has always found a more enthusiastic response in Latin America as a whole than adherence to political principles in the abstract. Iturriaga's emphasis on personal friendship seems to contradict what one of his own countrymen, Segura Millán, has written on the subject.[19] As for interest in social and political questions, Iturriaga's questionnaire reveals that this item ranked lowest (2.82%) in comparison with all other items. By contrast, interest in eroticism and pornography topped the list (34.34%)! Once again, several questions arise: How valid and reliable was this questionnaire, especially in view of the fact that it was conducted by radio? Who were the subjects? The date of the study is 1947. Would the results still hold true today?

Familiar items reappear. The Mexican is not given to reflection or analysis. Perhaps this is due to the fact that he is a product of two cultures, neither of which utilized reason to arrive at the truth. From the Indian he inherited the magic and the supernatural; from the Spaniard, a dogma which was imposed upon him. Yet this too can change; the advent of science is bound to have its repercussions, admits Iturriaga.[20] *Abulia* (lack of will), indecision, reluctance to accept responsibility, inability to carry through—all of these are related to his negative attitude toward a sense of time and punctuality. Time in the aboriginal culture was static and motionless; little or nothing occurred in it. In any case, fate always determines future events. The quick and easy way is preferable to hard work on long-term projects; hence the widespread popularity of the deeply-rooted institution known as the lottery (again—not restricted to Mexico!).

The Mexican improvises. This trait is, of course, present in other Hispanic countries as well, and is largely the result of a lack of specialization. The latter is characteristic of more developed countries. Improvisation frequently results in administrative disasters. Even though it may be picturesque and dramatic in certain respects, it, too, may be on the way out, due to the needs brought on by the progressively developing economy of the country. Seeking refuge in psychological compensation, the Mexican, who does not possess much, stresses quality rather than quantity, in contrast to the American who worships "bigness" (p. 243). This easy generalization is matched by another, equally controversial: in matters of religion, the Mexican is inclined to stress dogma and observe ritual, rather than emphasize the virtues of sound morality. On the other hand, the American prefers morality or social service to rites and ceremonies (p. 242).

Iturriaga offers a final word of caution: Mexicans residing in other parts of the country (i.e., not in the Federal District) are different: not all possess the characteristics outlined above. The inhabitant of Vera

---

[19] See above, p. 29.
[20] Iturriaga, p. 236.

Cruz, for example, is not timid or introvert; he speaks loudly.[21] His frankness and hospitality are akin to those of the Cuban or Venezuelan. The Mexican who lives in the northern area is energetic. (Has he, perhaps, been influenced by his powerful neighbour to the north?) The study concludes on an optimistic note. Many of the undesirable traits mentioned are likely to disappear as conditions change for the better. Mexico's vigorous national personality will, as a result, be redeemed, as the country ascends to a higher level of history (pp. 243-44).

Iturriaga's study can be said to be a "morphology" of the society and culture of twentieth-century Mexico. However, as González Casanova points out,[22] it does not penetrate sufficiently beneath the surface to explain the essence of society's struggles—its political, economic, social, **and cultural facets.** According to this criticism, the basic defect of all morphological studies is a lack of description and analysis of the forces which underlie observable manifestations. Iturriaga's study, then, is limited to what may be referred to as external description, without having reached any meaningful conclusions. Perhaps it might be more accurate to say that Iturriaga did not perform the kind of analysis or make predictions about Mexico's future course, which this critic would have preferred. The question, of course, is more basic: What kind of sociology are we dealing with? A treatise on descriptive sociology may or may not go into matters which are of primary concern to economists and political scientists. What seems to be a more serious defect in Iturriaga's work is a lack of consistency. On the one hand, he predicts optimistically that changing conditions will make for a diminution of "negative" traits. (They may also, conceivably, result in an increase or strengthening of these traits.) On the other, as he dwells on these characteristics, he considers them a cultural inheritance of the pre-Columbian and colonial periods. One may well ask: Haven't conditions changed since then? And, consequently, haven't some of these traits undergone modification? Shouldn't they have? Or are there some traits which are more resistant to change than others? More "innate" than others? In a similar vein, Béjar Navarro asks whether Mexican "inferiority" is still to be attributed to the fact that the Indians were vanquished by the Spaniards and that the less well-developed technical skills of the former, evident at the beginning of the Conquest, have lasted until well into the twentieth century.[23]

[21] See in this connection Carrión, "La sicología del veracruzano y la cultura," in *Mito y magia del mexicano*, pp. 96-108.

[22] Pablo González Casanova, "*La estructura social y cultural de México* by José Iturriaga," *Filosofía y Letras* 22, no. 43-44 (July-December 1951), 335-37.

[23] Béjar Navarro, p. 169.

CHAPTER THREE

LEOPOLDO ZEA

A. *On Mexican Traits*

Leopoldo Zea can perhaps be said to represent the apex of that entire group of intellectuals who, in the early 1950s, dedicated themselves to probing the so-called "essence" of the Mexican, and defining his identity. Zea approached the problem via the philosophic route in an attempt to discover the ingredients of Mexican identity, and on a broader scale, those of the Latin American "character"—if any can be said to exist.

In a lecture delivered in 1951,[1] Zea defines the term "history of culture" as the record of struggle involving man's attempt to define himself in the presence of his fellow man, and simultaneously, to define other men with respect to himself. Man wounds others and is wounded himself. In the process he develops a growing awareness of his human quality. While he utilizes objects as well as individuals in his attempt to give meaning to his environment, he also strives to have others recognize his own humanity. In short, man fights for recognition as a human being, while denying that same humanity to others (p. 193). He utilizes all sorts of pretexts to justify his exploitation: racial, sexual, and class factors. He speaks in the name of culture and civilization in order to enslave other people. In the process he becomes aware that human qualities do exist after all. As a result, he recognizes, perhaps reluctantly, the accidental nature of the differences which exist among men. More important for humanity are men's similarities—an optimistic assumption by Zea, one might add. Or as he puts it: "What is human is not that which separates or differentiates, but rather that which is similar" (p. 195)—and all this as a result of friction and strife.

Western culture, more than any other, has succeeded in projecting its point of view, and imposing it on other non-Western peoples. The view of Western man, which claims to be universal, has come to be accepted unquestioningly, complains Zea. It never occurred to anyone

[1] "Dialéctica de la conciencia en México," *La filosofía como compromiso* (Mexico: Tezontle, 1952).

to challenge this assumption, that is, until recently. Western man never felt the need to justify himself. His *Weltanschauung* was always considered the most superior form of human culture. Everything else was measured by Western standards of value. Englishmen, Frenchmen, Germans, etc., never questioned their identity, their very essence, as does the Mexican today. For they were not only Western; they were also, at least in their own minds, universal.

Recent crises have shaken this confidence. Crises have a way of pointing to the relativism of cultural values. Western man—especially in the twentieth century—has begun to recognize the existence of other points of view. The various peoples of the world who but yesterday were being imposed upon, subjugated, and dominated by the West, and who were, as a result, attempting to justify their own human condition, are today taking stock of their situation vis-à-vis the Western crisis. They no longer feel that they have to adopt the viewpoint of the West. They no longer need to borrow and imitate. They now can seek within themselves their own justification for being human. In other words, one no longer speaks of European or Western reality, as the only valid type of universality. What, for example, is the Chinese, Indian, Korean, Vietnamese, African, Mexican, or Brazilian circumstantial reality? What does each of these mean within the general context of reality, designated as "humanity"? Instead of imposition and domination, there is comprehension. So-called "accidents of history" are thus eliminated.

Perhaps if comprehension takes over, comprehension of others and especially of oneself—instead of domination and subjugation—then the Mexican will be on the way to ridding himself of all the negative characteristics which have been attributed to him, such as, for example, the oft-referred-to sense of inferiority and insufficiency, and the accompanying traits of resentment, hypocrisy, and cynicism. The Mexican, explains Zea, feels incomplete, amputated, and split. "We oscillate between two halves of our being. We feel obliged to choose between these two halves, rejecting one of them completely, and then trying to justify this rejection."[2]

Contemporary existentialism speaks of anguish and nausea as being characteristic of man today. Man feels himself shrinking to nothingness. The Mexican, by contrast, feels the need to add to himself, to supplement in order to make up for something which is missing. The Mexican does not feel that he is either expanding or shrinking; he is just divided, without seeing any possibility of joining the two halves. And this explains the phenomenon of imitation. Instead of striving to join these two inner halves of our being into a healthy whole, argues Zea, we look for a substitute outside of ourselves in other cultures.

[2] "El sentido de responsabilidad en el mexicano," *La filosofía como compromiso* (Mexico: Tezontle, 1952), p. 174.

Hence, the phenomenon of imitation, in the process of which we reflect our problems and concerns. This, in turn, causes us once more to turn inward upon ourselves in order to come face to face with our very being—only to escape from it again, seeking new models to imitate, and so on endlessly in an attempt to avoid the pain of the amputation, which we continue to perform upon ourselves when we choose one part of our being, with the consequent loss of the other (p. 175). The pain is a constant ingredient of our personality. It is always present whenever we have to make a choice. We always vacillate in the face of a decision. This makes for more insecurity and anxiety. And so we prefer to leave decision-making to others. The Mexican lives in a temporary, inconclusive, and incomplete world. "We try to act as little as possible in order to avoid the pain caused by the insufficiency of our action" (p. 176). The future, thus, appears as a means of evasion. It seems unrelated to both present and past, since time is also amputated. The past is what one would prefer not to have experienced; the present is something one must put up with. The past and present are therefore negative. Only the future is positive, but it is a future which cannot arrive because it is the opposite of the present. "It is a tomorrow which never arrives because in order to do so, it would have to transform itself into today, the present—that present which commits us, forcing us to decide" (p. 177). The future thus becomes a world of fantasy, the compensation for that constant failure which we experience.

Language helps out in this context. The "tomorrow" of the Mexican is tied to the present by means of a concept which can only be expressed as "inclination" or *gana*. Whenever we "feel like it," tomorrow will become today. The trouble is that this never happens, simply because "we don't feel like it." In this way, our evasion or irresponsibility finds its justification. We are what we are because we want to be that way, but the day we decide, we can be something else.

Irresponsibility (the term is rather strong, as employed by Zea) is what defines the plane of action. Choice implies responsibility and commitment. The trouble is that "we choose, but we do not wish to be responsible for our choice. We accept the future because we do not wish to be held accountable for our past" (p. 178).

As has been stated above, Samuel Ramos held that the origin of all these negative manifestations—inadequacy, inferiority, resentment, hypocrisy, and cynicism—was derived from the Spanish Conquest, a traumatic experience which might conceivably be pointed to in an attempt to justify irresponsibility. Zea enlarges upon this thesis. The sense of inferiority, he claims, although inherited from colonial times, came to the surface and appeared to be much more obvious after Independence, when Mexico came in contact with the Western culture of the nineteenth century. It was then that the Mexican realized his backwardness, especially in view of the frustration experienced at not being able to attain the ideals of nineteenth-century liberalism. Mexico aspired to live at the same level as other nations, but to its dismay it found that its colonial past proved to be too great an obstacle. This was especially painful for the Mexican because he claimed that he had had no part in the development of his past. This was a past in which he had been told to keep silent and obey, a past from which he sought to remove himself. This was the source of his weaknesses, his inability, his failures, and kept him from achieving the same cultural level as that attained by other peoples of the Western World (pp. 179-81).

The Mexican feels ashamed, considering his actions imperfect. His projects are failures before he even initiates them. He therefore compensates for this inadequacy by setting up special categories which he believes will give him "status" in the eyes of the "outside world." For example, in philosophy, he will consider as legitimate only those problems which can be labelled "universal," "eternal," or "permanent." Mexican problems are taboo for him; he is afraid to discuss concrete truths which characterize his circumstance. Or if he consents to deal with them, he will give them an "abstract" flavour (p. 184).

Are we, then, really inferior? asks Zea. Are we condemned to build castles in the air and nothing else? No, he retorts vigorously. Such an attitude would imply that we suffer from something much worse than a mere disease. It would mean that we have ceased being men, and that we have lost that most important attribute which characterizes man, namely freedom: the ability to make a choice even in the most difficult of circumstances. There are other countries, Zea insists, which are smaller and weaker than we are, countries with fewer possibilities of action, in which these negative characteristics do not appear. Inferiority is not a consequence of being unable to achieve in circumstances which make such achievement unlikely or impossible. It is, rather, the result of not achieving that which lies within our reach. It is precisely because we feel ourselves capable, that we have reacted so negatively in the face of what we consider a failure (pp. 185-86).

Another trait which Zea criticizes is pride. Pride prevents the Mexican from developing projects he should never have undertaken in the first place. Mexico's past is responsible for wounded pride. To erase this past was the task of the nineteenth century. We tried without success to replace our discarded past, Zea reminds his audience, to repair our truncated being by attempting to emulate the political and educational models of the powerful neighbour to the north. But in vain! We keep on being the same. What we were did not coincide with what we wanted to be. Our projects did not conform to changed conditions. And so, out of pride we blame history, blood, race, and environment for our failures. But we refuse to change our projects. Instead of realizing ourselves culturally and materially in accordance with our possibilities, we prefer to lament because we cannot be equal to or greater than Europe or the United States. And since we cannot be like them, we prefer to be nothing. "Instead of creating, we prefer to imitate" (p. 188).

It is for these reasons that the Mexican does not speak in terms of "subjective" or "relative" elements—which would be more in keeping with his reality. Instead, he prefers to deal with "universal" terms, created supposedly by those nations that have risen to power and have aroused his envy. Envy leads to imitation and as a result, the Mexican arrives at the "universal" through alien efforts and channels instead of his own.

Zea therefore insists—and eloquently so—that the Mexican is the author of his own way of life, and that he can now choose to alter his identity, his personality structure, by adopting positive attitudes, provided, of course, that he change his life projects. He must begin by assuming responsibility for his *situation*, instead of trying to evade it. Part of the stock-taking process consists in realizing that the projects of his forebears cannot be *his* projects. The situation, the circumstances and the possibilities are not identical. Facing up to this is not a sign of inferiority. This new perspective will result in a change of attitudes: from negative to positive. The Mexican will become increasingly aware that ability is not related to race. Only then will he realize that one can arrive at universality via channels other than those of imitation (p. 191).

* * * * *

More than two decades ago, Zea wrote: "Mexicanism in itself, cannot be a legitimate goal, but only a point of departure, a means toward a broader and more responsible task."[3] At that time Zea undertook the task of analyzing additional facets of the Mexican personality. The Mexican, he stated, has a concrete sense of political relationships. He enters into these relationships with individuals, rather than operate on an abstract level with the government. Personal connections serve to heighten interest. Obtaining a government position, for example, is possible only as a result of promoting these personal bonds. The Mexican is inclined to fight and die, if necessary, for a *caudillo*, rather than an ideal. This personal loyalty is imperative in a society in which individuals have to struggle daily with a difficult and hostile circumstance (p. 47). The president of the country is viewed as the Great Provider of necessities, distributed personally. In fact, anyone who operates in impersonal, abstract terms is viewed with suspicion. Mexicans, according to Zea, project their allegiance passionately toward a leader, rather than the law. This highly subjective form of political behaviour suffered traumatically as a result of abuses, deceptions, and

---

[3] *Conciencia y posibilidad del mexicano* (Mexico: Porrúa y Obregón, 1952), p. 23.

disappointments throughout Mexican history. What emerged, as a result, was a resentful individual, suspicious, timid, and unreliable as concerns any kind of political action which might go beyond his immediate interests. All activity was directed exclusively toward the satisfaction of the here and now. Because of disappointing experiences in the past, any long-term project produced only cynicism and hypocrisy. The Mexican, therefore, maintains a constant reserve, a "wait-and-see" attitude; his confidence is always tentative and provisional, depending upon promises which are never kept. This lack of confidence is, thus, a permanent condition. No one feels responsible for anything or anyone (pp. 49-50). The citizen's loyalty to the government is predicated on the latter's ability to keep promises. This necessitates satisfying some, but in the process, disappointing others, or at least holding out some hope for them "next time."

The Mexican Revolution crystallized this social and psychological reality, this "lying in wait" type of morality. The Revolution had to attend to immediate needs. Practical men with cynical attitudes had to "deliver." Until the present moment, claims Zea, the Mexican had been "practical" and "immediate." However, now, more than half a century after the Revolution, it becomes necessary to seek rational bases to justify this former "immediacy," to establish theoretical guidelines for the Mexican's behaviour, and to suggest and develop solutions to the manifold problems which continue to face the nation.

In the course of wrestling with these problems, the Mexican should beware of falling into any more traps, such as adopting utopian schemes which do not fit national circumstances. Above all, he should adopt programs which he can deal with realistically and responsibly, and in accord with his possibilities and abilities. Utopias can only lead to irresponsibility, as they have in the past (pp. 54-55).

The possibilities of the Mexican's self-realization, once actualized, will lead him along the road toward a greater degree of commonality with other peoples, or in other words, universality. For example, since the unexpected is the usual pattern of existence for the Mexican, it is not surprising that anxiety, insecurity, and inconsistency should constitute the basic ingredients of a permanent way of life. The Mexican can offer his example to other peoples who follow a similar pattern, as a possible solution to their problems, especially in view of the fact that this all-pervasive anxiety has not destroyed his love of life nor his creative powers. In fact, this propensity for "living dangerously" or, as Zea puts it, this insecurity which expresses itself in the form of "disinterestedness" is what makes real creativity possible (pp. 88-89). One suspects at this point that Zea is indulging in a bit of wishful thinking, or at least, that he is romanticizing. Negative characteristics are viewed through rose-tinted spectacles. This impression is reinforced, especially by Zea's discussion of the Mexican's relationship to technology. The Mexican is not overpowered or victimized by the machine. Unlike the situation which prevails in Europe and the United States, where the machine has dehumanized man, the Mexican "has until now humanized the machine" (p. 100). In other words, there is a personal relationship between the two. One wonders whether Zea still holds to this opinion, given the increased tempo of industrialization experienced by Mexico since the above was written. Also, the phrase "until now" would lead one to suspect that Zea himself may have his doubts. Yet one should not criticize too severely. Zea has entitled this section of his discussion "the Mexican as Possibility"—possibility for philosophical meditations, the result of which would serve as a contribution to universal thought, as was the case, for example, with Greek, French, German, and British meditations. Yet in spite of this praiseworthy objective, one cannot help but take exception to the apparently over-simplified (and again, romanticized) contrast presented between the Mexican and other peoples of the Western World. In other countries, claims Zea, man is a slave to his wealth. In Mexico, possessions are accidental; they are merely instrumentalities in the service of other goals. The Mexican does not save his money. He works only to earn what is necessary in order to satisfy his daily requirements. This is so because he leads a hazardous existence, independent of material circumstances. Which Mexican is Zea referring to? is a logical question. In the West, he continues, the individual has become a robot, a statistic. His personality is jeopardized by a society in which every action of his is calculated with mathematical precision. By contrast, the Mexican's way of life is not depersonalized or computerized. It is more human, and is based on personal contacts. Favours are obtained through the good offices of friends or relatives, or friends of friends—a culture pattern that bears the name *amiguismo* (pp. 102-103).

The trouble is, complains Zea, that we have been compared and evaluated according to norms established in the West. In other words, the measuring devices are "culture-biased." The precarious economic condition of Mexico combined with the cultural progress of the West have tended to exaggerate the value of foreign norms. Zea seems to be criticizing Ramos' study which applied the Adlerian concept of the inferiority complex to an analysis of Mexican character. This partiality with respect to norms (praising "theirs" and denigrating "ours") has blinded us to the positive elements in our behaviour and the negative components in theirs. We have failed to take into account our diverse circumstances (p. 105).

But since World War II an inversion of values seems to have taken place. Mexican behaviour patterns, insists Zea, do not appear to be so negative after all! They can actually be positive, if adjusted to the demands of our reality, in relation to our personality. Western culture is seeking in other cultures behaviour patterns which could vitalize it, and lend new elasticity to its mechanized forms of moral and social action. This development has enabled Europe to better understand and appreciate the cultures of other peoples. It has also made it possible for Mexicans to re-evaluate their own. Implied in all this is man's capacity to adapt and re-adapt himself to circumstances—an area in which the Mexican has had ample experience. Facing the unexpected is nothing new for him; yet it is the first such experience for other peoples, especially for those of the non-Western world. However, the Mexican's primary need, at the moment, is to develop an awareness which will dissipate and render unnecessary all complexes and resentments which he may harbour in the process of dealing with the unexpected. Zea sees the development of such awareness as an urgent task for the philosopher (pp. 106-107). Furthermore, since the non-Western nations have been catapulted into the realization that they, too, should participate in a value system which had its origin in the West, it would seem to Zea that Mexico, indeed all of Latin America, has its philosophic task carved out for itself: to become a bridge between the Western and non-Western worlds.

B. The Philosophical Approach

The question as to whether or not Latin America can develop its own so-called ideology, an autonomous philosophy with its own peculiar stamp, one not patterned necessarily upon European currents of thought, and also whether such a philosophy might contribute to European culture, has occupied Zea for the past several decades. In the early forties he broached the subject of whether such an American philosophy is possible, thinking primarily in terms of Latin America.[4]

The existence or nonexistence of a specifically Latin American culture in general, and a philosophy in particular, was to run like a continuous thread throughout his later writings, and be further developed and viewed from a variety of perspectives, enriched by the passage of time and changing circumstances.

Zea begins his discussion by stating that the theme has its origin in our time. It has practically forced itself upon the Latin American intellectual who had, until the period between the two World Wars, felt secure within a culture that spoke in terms of universality, and was valid for all time. The crisis undergone by Western society since then, especially in the interval which followed the Second World War, convinced the Latin American of his error. The culture in which he had placed his faith seemed to him to have come apart. He was therefore faced with

---

[4] Zea's essay ("En torno a una filosofía americana") first appeared in *Cuadernos Americanos* (May-June 1942), and was subsequently published in book form: *En torno a una filosofía americana* (Mexico: El Colegio de México, 1945).

the necessity of creating and cultivating his own system of ideas and beliefs. The problem had thus imposed itself; the Latin American was no longer free to choose his themes. Instead, themes were impinging themselves upon him (pp. 16-17).

The European crisis, then, had made it necessary to develop an American culture. Latin America had all along imitated European culture only because such imitation had best served its interests. However, Europe itself had now become a problem, and could no longer be depended upon. Its ideas were a hindrance, rather than a help. It had failed to recognize that other cultures which it had all along designated as "marginal" also possessed "humanity" and operated according to certain value systems. Latin America represented one of these "marginal" areas.

Was America, i.e., Latin America, a mere shadow of Europe, as Hegel had claimed? Not at all, protests Zea. In the past, the continent had been compelled to solve its problems in accordance with its circumstance, with the means afforded it by that circumstance. In most cases these means had been utilized by Europe and had sufficed for America. In this respect America had indeed been an echo. But now this was no longer adequate. As a result of the crisis experienced by the Western World, there were no longer any satisfactory solutions that could be offered by Europe and utilized by Latin America. Europe had itself become a problem, a burden rather than a source of aid. Hence, imitation of European culture was now obliged to give way to Latin American inventiveness and creativity. This was imperative, since not only Europe, but also the "echo," were threatened, culturally speaking. Apparently old remedies did not seem to work any more, hence new solutions had to be found. The conclusion arrived at by Zea—and this is his basic theme and point of departure—was that America needed a philosophy, one which implied fresh thinking and original solutions to its problems (p. 19). Such a philosophy would be the result of having to solve urgent vital problems; it would be produced when necessary. In the past, maintains Zea, we have philosophized only because we have wanted to show "that we are not inferior" (p. 22).

For Zea philosophy is historic truth. Obviously inspired by Ortega, Zea argues that philosophy is the work of man and what is human in man, i.e., his very essence is history. Man is thus an historic entity whose essence is change. He is always situated in a definite circumstance which appears in the form of a problem, a circumstance which also offers the means of solving that problem. The end result of man's adaptation to his circumstance is culture. In short, the history of culture is that of man engaged in a struggle with his circumstance (p. 26).

What is at times considered a solution may in other circumstances be an obstacle. The change in generations may be a crucial factor. It is, therefore, evident that there is an intimate relationship between ideas and historical circumstances on the one hand, and so-called "contradictions" in the history of philosophy, on the other. Solutions for one generation, people, or culture are not always feasible for other peoples and cultures. The history of philosophy, therefore, appears lacking in unity. The attempts by individual philosophers to lay claim to the Absolute Truth have resulted in a history of philosophical contradictions. Only in this way can one explain the fact that man has existed so long with a plurality of truths, instead of one eternal truth.

One of the most serious errors committed by Mexicans (and Latin Americans, generally) has been the failure to realize that solutions to problems are particular, rather than universal. Adopting European solutions has left Americans ill adapted to their circumstance. Each generation or national group attempts to change its world in accord with a conception of life which it considers characteristically its own. It views its truths not as relative solutions to problems, but as absolute and valid for all time and place. For that particular group its reality is absolute—as are its point of view and its conception of the world. Utilizing Orteguian perspectivism, Zea goes on to say that what is not absolute is the position or situation which each individual or group occupies in reality (p. 30).

One might even improve upon Zea's formulation and argue that increased fragmentation of the truth is possible for the same generation. The "truths" and solutions of a given generation are not necessarily uniform and "absolute," as Zea maintains. Conflicts exist not only between generations, but also within the same age group: hence different truths because of variable circumstances, even at the same time and place. This difficulty would seem to be compounded, when one considers a national group, a people, or certainly an entire continent, namely, Latin America.

Yet even though Zea rejects the idea of philosophy as eternal truth, he avoids the pitfall at the other extreme, namely, a narrowly relativistic approach, by introducing what seems to be a comfortable synthesis: philosophy as "absolute circumstantial truth." There are, he admits, truths which are valid for all men. This is understood if we remember that man operates within a personal circumstance which is also part of a wider context—one in which many individuals participate, i.e., the social circumstance. Furthermore, the latter, in turn, evolves into a still wider area, wherein all men—regardless of their individual or social circumstances—identify with one another. This last is the human circumstance, or humanity at large (p. 31).

Philosophy deals with this human circumstance. Ideally, it tries to solve problems of a universal scale. However, man, who creates this philosophy, is himself incapable of realizing these universal solutions, simply because his individual and social circumstances of time and place combine to form an obstacle which conditions the process. The

Greeks, for example, attempted to develop a philosophy for all men, but were conditioned by their circumstances. It is not that the Greeks self-consciously set out to create a Greek philosophy. They simply solved problems arising out of their circumstances, with an eye to offering their solutions to all men. The limits and obstacles which lay in their path conditioned their thought and stamped it with Greek circumstantiality. Only in this sense was Greek philosophy bequeathed to the world.

In the same way, according to Zea, Latin American philosophy will have to be the result of a desire to solve human problems. It is not enough to wish to deal exclusively with American problems (p. 34). This approach will not, in and of itself, produce an American philosophy. The American coloration will emerge in spite of our attempt to achieve universal validity. The human quality will ipso facto make that philosophy circumstantial, and hence, American. It will achieve a certain measure of universal value by virtue of the fact that it will have been made by men, and determined by what Americans have in common with their fellow-man. Circumstantial limitations will determine the "American" contribution to the problems of man in general, and therefore, of universal culture.

Granted, then, that circumstances are limits which prevent one from attaining universal truths, and that, moreover, one must nevertheless strive to overcome these obstacles in the search for solutions to problems which arise. The question is: What are these peculiar circumstances which characterize the Latin American scene? What is the American reality?

In considering the problem, one must take as a point of departure the relationship between Latin America and Europe, more specifically the former's cultural dependence upon the latter. Ours is a culture, declares Zea, "which we do not consider our own in view of the fact that we long for an American culture" (p. 40). Latin America has utilized European culture by imitating it, and has accepted European solutions for American problems. These have been found wanting. Zea wants his country (and his continent) to solve its own problems. But how? Some of his compatriots would go so far as to break with Western culture—a step which Zea opposes. The trouble is, he states, that we are aware of the fact that European culture is not ours, but if we seek to discover that which we can truly call our own, we cannot find it (p. 43).

Nor is Latin America to be compared with Asia in this respect. In the case of the East, only the superficial aspects of European culture, such as technology, have been assimilated. A way of life, a conception of the world—these have not been adopted. The Asians consider themselves heirs of a culture which has passed from father to son; hence, they feel that they are the possessors of their own culture.

Can the same be said for Latin Americans? Unlike the people of Asia, Zea feels that his fellow Americans do not consider that they have inherited an autochthonous culture. True, there existed an indigenous American culture—Aztec, Maya, Inca, etc.—but this does not hold the same meaning for Latin Americans as that which the ancient Oriental cultures have for Asians, even though there are many Mexicans today who are proud of their Aztec heritage. It should be added parenthetically that Zea, as a Mexican, certainly cannot equate his cultural position vis-à-vis the Aztecs, for example, with that of the Argentinian or the Chilean. In short, one cannot speak of the Latin Americans as though they were a homogeneous, undifferentiated group. It is true, as Zea asserts, that Mexicans are the result of a *mestizaje*, but the pre-Columbian culture has no meaning for them. Ours (to paraphrase Zea once more) is not a father-son relationship, which is the case in Asia. We feel more like bastards than like legitimate sons (p. 44). We do not feel that the European culture which we have borrowed is really ours. We utilize the benefits of European civilization with a feeling of guilt, as though we had no right to them. Ours is a sense of alienation and inadaptation. The trouble, Zea continues, is that we Mexicans want to adapt to European culture, instead of vice versa. The European beliefs and doctrines are ours, but not the circumstances which gave birth to those beliefs and nurtured them. We have our own circumstances. These we try to fit into European values, a process which amounts to adjusting reality to ideas instead of the contrary (p. 45). And if our American circumstances do not conform, so much the worse for them! Yet America cannot be transformed into a second Europe. It has to make its own history and forge its own destiny. As a result of constant borrowing and imitation, the Latin American has developed feelings of frustration and inferiority. What is distinctly American is considered inferior because Europe is "superior." One wonders at this point whether Zea is not perhaps projecting toward the rest of the continent that which may be partially true only among certain Mexicans.

What, then, is the source of this difficulty, this reluctance by the American to write his own history? To discover the answer, Zea takes us back to the period of the discovery of the New World. America, the daughter of European culture, was born during one of the great crises of the Old World. Europe was driven to discover America. The European's religious faith was no longer sufficient for him. His world had come crashing down. He needed new ideals and beliefs, and new places on the map with which to associate these beliefs. America seemed most suitable. The European could now initiate in the new land of promise all that he could not, or dared not, realize in his native country.

America (again: Zea means Latin America), virgin territory, land of possibility, was thus a projection of European ideals, of dreams to be fulfilled. America had no past, no tradition, only a future. The trouble was that neither the projects nor the future were its own; they were European. Europe saw in America a utopia of what it wanted America to be. Upon not finding it, the European felt disappointed. The result? Alienation of the European (now the new American) from his reality; an alienation brought about by his refusal to recognize that he had his own circumstance. The American, maintains Zea, has refused to recognize that he has a history. History for the American has consisted of a desire to live in the future, blotting out the past, and building a utopia for the European; in short, not to be an American (p. 51).

Now America has finally turned inward upon itself and is looking for its tradition—a tradition which consists of refusals and denials— neither European nor pre-Columbian. America represents a value for Europe, Europe's future, but the American does not know what kind of future it will be. As a result, the American experiences a feeling of impotence and an inferiority complex.

This is not true of Latin America alone. Anglo-America, too, suffers from this complex. It boasts of being the future of Western culture, of attempting to be a "bigger and better Europe" by means of wealth and technology. But deep inside itself it knows it cannot; technical skill is not the equivalent of cultural capacity. And so North America, too, experiences feelings of inferiority for which it strives to compensate with the mask of "bigness" (p. 52).

By contrast, the Latin American does not hide his feeling of inferiority. He exhibits it constantly, parades it publicly, and continues to denigrate himself. At this point Zea seems to coincide with Samuel Ramos. The Latin American is always planning something for which he is not prepared. The result, inevitably, is failure. He does not attribute this failure, as he should, to the dissonance between goals and circumstances, but rather to what he believes is innate incapacity (p. 54). Consequently, he is incapable of evaluating himself. His lack of confidence and fear of ridicule make it impossible for him to undertake anything by himself. Since he is afraid to make mistakes, he prefers to imitate. Devoid of ideals, he has neither a past nor a future. What matters is today—to live as best he can. Egotism is a corollary of inferiority feelings. Social ideals do not count; what is more important are personal interests (p. 55). This would account for a lack of a sense of nationality. And there is no sense of nationality because there has not been any awareness of truly American phenomena.

Such is Zea's devastating analysis. Yet he does not stop there. Like Ramos before him, he wishes to end on a constructive note. He therefore disagrees with his distinguished countryman, Alfonso Reyes, who implies that being American is unfortunate, in the sense of having been born on an outpost of civilization, a sort of "commercial branch office of Europe."[5] But this is not so bad, retorts Zea. Being born has given us

[5] Reyes, *Ultima Tule*, p. 89.

the possibility of affirming a personality, far different from that of a mere echo. We have a body and a voice. We can function within a universal culture to which we can contribute by way of new kinds of human experiences. By all means, let us eschew the position of the extreme nationalist: that of denying any affinity with Europe. This would be an untenable stance. Whether we like it or not, we are children of European culture, but we have our own personality which differentiates us from our cultural forebears. By being aware of our true relationship with this culture, we can eliminate all feeling of inferiority. In its place we would develop a sense of responsibility. Only then will we "come of age," as Reyes has written. And coming of age implies recognition of the fact that the Latin American does have a past which he does not have to disown. At this mature stage he should no longer have to be ashamed of having had a childhood. Only then, too, will he be part of history, claiming his place in Western culture and collaborating therein. What is most important is that he will then be able to solve his problems by himself, and in the process, solve those of all of Western culture insofar as he is linked to them.[6]

What, exactly, are the tasks which the Latin American philosopher should impose upon himself? What are the problems to be posed in order to philosophize legitimately? Zea stresses the need to be concerned with problems of a universal nature, i.e., those which are related to *all* men. Latin Americans, too, are men. Yet their solutions, born of particular circumstances, although perhaps not valid for all times, may conceivably be useful for other men as well. The fact that we may not yet have a philosophy which we may properly call our own, maintains Zea, does not exclude the possibility that we may eventually have one when we experience the need to bring it into being. It certainly does not imply that we are incapable of philosophizing. It is only recently that we have begun to replace our sense of inferiority with a healthy attitude as concerns our positive cultural development. The sense of maturity we experience will eliminate our resentment and make us more responsible (p. 62).

Our philosophy, Zea reminds us, will continue the study of themes not yet solved by European culture: Being, Knowledge, Space, Time, God, Life, Death, etc. These abstract themes will have to be viewed within the framework of reality peculiar to the American. Different solutions for these problems merely reveal the national, and perhaps even continental, stamp. For it must not be forgotten that despite the desire for universality, philosophers differ from one another, precisely because they bear the imprint of their respective circumstances. Thus we have a Greek philosophy, a Christian philosophy, a French philosophy, an English philosophy, and a German philosophy (p. 63).

[6] Zea, *Filosofía americana*, p. 57.

Mexicans and Latin Americans have a series of problems peculiar to their own reality. The mere fact that Mexico has produced poor copies of European philosophical systems indicates that Mexico has tried to be what it is not. There is thus a positive lesson to be learned from the reproduction of "poor copies," namely, that Mexico is not inferior, but simply different. In this poor copy, perhaps, is imbedded Mexico's essence which it is looking for but does not want to behold (pp. 65-66).

Where is this "essence," this reality, to be found? What is its nature? Zea believes that the key lies in a study of history, specifically the history of ideas. A knowledge of historical circumstances is indispensable for the longed-for maturation process which will hopefully result in increased responsibility. Zea places Mexico within the framework of America and situates America within the context of history. There are, of course, other perspectives as well. Besides philosophy and history, distinguished members of Zea's generation have also dealt with the problem from the standpoint of sociology, psychology, and literature.[7] The political philosopher, too, makes this one of the primary objects of study. To cite one example: the State must insure a stable equilibrium between the individual and social components in order to avoid either anarchy or totalitarianism. This balance requires philosophical justification; hence, it is not unusual for metaphysical abstractions to culminate in systems of ethics and politics (pp. 72-73). Humanity, then, must have ideas to justify actions. Theory and practice should be complementary.

The trouble is that the present era is witness to a breakdown in the relationship between theory and practice. World War II and its aftermath provide the background for Zea's thesis. Man in Western culture, he maintains, has tried to explain his actions without any moral justification. The present crisis is the result of the triumph of brute force. There has been a rupture between the metaphysical and the political planes of operation. Yet in reply to Zea, one is tempted to enter a caveat: immoral acts are not restricted to the here and now. Three centuries ago Thomas Hobbes pointed out that man is still a wolf, and that life is "nasty" and "brutish."

Modern man seems left to his own impulses; he is without orientation and devoid of ideas and values which should serve as models or give purpose to his acts. When ideas fail to justify reality, the latter loses its human sense, and then it becomes necessary to seek out new ideas and values which will perform that function.[8] If reality tends to change,

----

[7] The quest for Mexican identity has found expression in numerous literary works. Carlos Fuentes in the novel (*La región más transparente*) and Rodolfo Usigli in the theatre (*El gesticulador*) are but two examples of this tendency. Both authors attempt to interpret Mexican essence in terms of the significance of the Revolution of 1910. A critical evaluation of their work, as well as that of other Mexican authors in this respect, lies outside the confines of this study.

[8] Zea, *Filosofía americana*, p. 74.

ideals and ideal justifications which undergird this reality should also be modified. This is the task of the intellectual. However, if the latter chooses to shut himself up in an ivory tower and thus betray his responsibility, there will be no new ideas to keep pace with the changing reality.

The entire history of Western culture is the history of the crises which men have undergone when coordination between ideas and reality was destroyed. Western culture has gone from crisis to crisis, finding salvation sometimes in Platonic Ideas, sometimes in God, sometimes in Reason. Today it finds itself without any of these (p. 75).

The contemporary Western World, then, is in the process of seeking new values upon which to base itself. These new values and ideas will be derived from new circumstances and new human experiences. Possibly some of the latter may have been ignored by the West. Since Latin America is part of Western culture, it may conceivably make an authentic contribution in order to prevent man's dehumanization, by bringing to this culture the novelty and value of its experiences. Latin America is, therefore, in a privileged position at the moment, one which should be seized upon in order to implement the task which has fallen to it. Only in this way will she "come of age" and take her proper place within Western culture (pp. 77-78).

In the process of forging this philosophical contribution, it must be remembered that the thinking that will go into it will not confine itself to problems peculiarly American. It will, instead, attempt to embrace a broader reality. It is not enough to attain an American truth; one should strive to attain a truth valid for all men, even though this may never be possible. To create an American philosophy with the sole aspiration that it be American is a project doomed to failure. One must simply try to produce philosophy. The American component or essence will emerge, for good measure, like it or not. Mexico and Latin America in general, taking their respective realities as a point of departure, will yet hammer out a philosophy with its own particular coloration, in spite of themselves.

* * * * *

Zea's early research into the development of Positivism in Mexico and the rest of Latin America is an attempt to establish a working relationship between Latin American philosophy and the history of ideas on the continent. His *Dos etapas*[9] aspires to capture the process of intellectual development of the entire continent within the period indicated (from Romanticism to Positivism). This work may be considered an elaboration and extension of earlier efforts, that is, to per-

[9] Leopoldo Zea, *Dos etapas del pensamiento en Hispanoamérica* (Mexico: El Colegio de México, 1949).

form for Latin America what he had done for Mexico.[10] Zea himself has stated that in view of the way in which Mexico had reacted to Positivism, it would be interesting, from a comparative point of view, to examine the reaction to this movement by other countries of Latin America.

Zea has always believed that the essence of the Mexican, indeed of the Spanish American in general—his ambivalence and conflicts—is best illustrated in the interval which embraces Romanticism and Positivism. For it is during this period that the Spanish American felt himself divided in two, truncated as it were, without any hope of ever being put together again. The cause of it all was the profound conflict in his mind between two ways of life: on the one hand, the borrowed element in his culture, or worse, that which had been imposed upon him from without in the course of three centuries of colonial rule, and on the other, his own "value" system, still uncertain and problematical, which he was trying to work out and arrive at—often through the most violent means. In other words, we are dealing here with a transition period from which, incidentally it seems, the Latin American has not yet emerged in spite of all efforts to the contrary.[11] This was a stage which presented problems, the solutions to which have still to be discovered; an era, moreover, in which can be found the roots of both the virtues and defects of the Latin American.

Zea's discussion of Latin American reality in connection with Positivism led him to a consideration of the philosophical possibilities of the continent, and thence to a series of meditations concerning some of the more recent problems of Latin American culture. Many of his works represent an amplification of themes dealt with in earlier volumes, and an attempt to unify them into a single, comprehensive whole. For example, the philosophy of Mexicanness would tend to lead directly to the philosophy of Latin Americanism, assuming of course that such a philosophy exists. Zea's hope has always been to have similar works appear, dealing with the history of ideas as this affects each Latin American country, and applying philosophic concepts to the concrete reality of that country. Since then, an impressive number of volumes have been published, which deal with philosophic thought and the history of ideas in individual countries.[12] Zea has thus enlarged his

[10] Leopoldo Zea, *El positivismo en México* (1st ed., Mexico: El Colegio de México, 1943); *Apogeo y decadencia del positivismo en México* (1st ed., Mexico: El Colegio de México, 1944).

[11] See in this connection Arturo Ardao, "Un enfoque mexicano del positivismo uruguayo," *Marcha* (Montivideo, Uruguay), December 30, 1949.

[12] Guillermo Francovich, *El pensamiento boliviano en el siglo XX* (1956); Arturo Ardao, *Espiritualismo y positivismo en el Uruguay* (1956) and *La filosofía en el Uruguay en el siglo XX* (1956); João Cruz Costa, *Esbozo de una historia de las ideas en el Brasil* (1957); Augusto Salazar Bondy, *Historia de las ideas en el Perú contemporáneo* (1965); Ricardo Donoso, *Las ideas políticas en Chile* (1946); José Luis Romero, *Las ideas políticas en Argentina* (1946); Rafael Heliodoro Valle, *Historia de las ideas contemporáneas en Centro América* (1960); Constantino Láscaris, *Historia de las ideas en Centro América* (1970); Monelosa Lina

perspective and has travelled in an outward direction in terms of what may be conceived of as a series of concentric circles: from Mexico to Latin America which he eventually places within the context of Western culture, the relationship which the continent bears to the Third World, and finally, the dynamic interaction among all concerned.[13]

In his early work on Mexican Positivism Zea develops the thesis that the new bourgeoisie needed a philosophical justification with which to defend its class interests. The social disorder caused by the activities of the so-called Jacobins, their conflicts with the clergy and the military, were not calculated to produce the sort of stability required by the emerging middle class. Comtian Positivism was therefore brought into the country, conceived of as a means of putting an end to eternal conflict by establishing a hierarchical classification of thought—a task undertaken by the educator, Gabino Barreda. The situation was thus parallel to what had occurred in France. Wasn't Comtism the antidote to the disorder produced by the French Revolution? Comtian Positivism thus seemed to be the new ideology, adopted by the bourgeoisie, in order to advance its position. After the triumph of Benito Juárez it had stressed "order" and group harmony as an answer to the liberal Jacobins who had placed the emphasis upon freedom. However, when this same bourgeoisie felt the need to expand its own economic activities, it began to lay greater stress upon freedom, but this time bearing in mind the individual's propensity to enrich himself in the name of "progress." It was at this point that Spencerian Positivism replaced the Comtian variety. The terms "order" and "progress," then, which constituted the keynote of Positivism, did not necessarily go hand-in-hand. Very often they ran counter to each other. In the Mexican case, each component was merely emphasized at a different historical moment to suit the occasion.

"Order" was to lead eventually to the establishment of the Díaz dictatorship, just as "freedom," in the second phase, was to become the main slogan for the country's progress in the platform of the *científicos*—a group which soon found itself heading on a collision course with Porfirio Díaz.

In similar fashion, Zea delves into the historical framework of each Latin American country and shows the use to which Positivism was put in accordance with the national circumstance. In Argentina, for example, it was a weapon, used to combat "barbarism" and introduce "civilization." Some Argentines even tried to effect a synthesis between Spencerian Positivism and a revised Marxism. The Chileans considered Positivism (which split into two wings, the orthodox and the

Pérez-Marchand, *Historia de las ideas en Puerto Rico* (1960) and *Desarrollo de las ideas en Costa Rica*, 2nd ed., 1975).

[13] See Francisco Romero, "El americanismo filosófico de Leopoldo Zea," *La Prensa* (Buenos Aires), July 27, 1958.

heterodox) as the road leading toward liberalism. In Uruguay Positivism was a means of putting an end to corruption and military coups; in Peru and Bolivia, an instrumentality utilized to regain confidence and achieve rehabilitation after the disastrous war against Chile. Finally, in Cuba, it was a doctrine (the Spencerian, rather than the Comtian brand) which justified the patriots' yearning for independence from Spain. In short, Spanish Americans saw in Positivism a doctrine of salvation, a means with which to change reality. For the Brazilians, by contrast, it was an instrument with which to further advance an already existent reality.

To summarize, Latin American Positivism, according to Zea, was adopted by countries attempting to achieve modernization. From Comte they took the concept of organic social evolution and the primacy of society, as opposed to the individual. On the other hand, Spencer's social dynamics also proved appealing, together with its corollary: the emphasis on the individual.

Yet Zea comes in for his share of criticism. One critic charges him with lack of sufficient documentation.[14] Neither the philosopher nor the historian will be satisfied. Such seems to be the fate of the "history of ideas" or the "philosophy of history." Another critic suggests that Zea has failed to detail the national "urgencies" and "historical circumstances" which shaped the adaptation of Positivism to each country studied. Questions such as the following remain unanswered: Why did Mexican Positivism come to an end with the Revolution of 1910? Why did Brazil—the only country that did so—accept the religious aspect of Comtian Positivism, namely, the "religion of humanity"? Why did Positivism lead to the founding of the Argentine Socialist Party?[15]

However, a much more serious and comprehensive criticism of Zea's approach to historiography comes from Raat, who claims that Zea is actually more speculative than historical in the empirical sense.[16] For example, Zea, according to this critic, tries to overemphasize the role of the intellectual in society in his treatment of the overthrow of Positivism. Zea was, no doubt, referring in this connection to the activities of the Mexican *Ateneo*, whose membership boasted of such luminaries as Alfonso Reyes, José Vasconcelos, Antonio Caso and Pedro Henríquez Ureña. Furthermore, Raat goes on to say, Zea does not employ a sociological approach in his study of Positivism. There is no attempt made to analyze Mexican institutions, such as the role of the

[14] Alfonso García Ruiz, "El positivismo en México," *Revista de Historia de América* 16 (December 1943), 221-23.

[15] See Stanley J. Stein, review of *The Latin American Mind*, a translation of Zea's *Dos etapas del pensamiento en Hispanoamérica* by James B. Abbott and Lowell Dunham (Norman: University of Oklahoma Press, 1963), in *Political Science Quarterly* 80 (March 1965), 156.

[16] William D. Raat, "Leopoldo Zea and Mexican Positivism: A Reappraisal," *The Hispanic American Historical Review* 48, no. 1 (February 1968). The same article appears in Spanish translation in *Latino América* 2 (1969).

Catholic Church or that of the group of *científicos*. For example, Zea asks "What is a Mexican?" instead of "What is the social status of the so-called Mexican positivist?" (p. 12)—a point, incidentally, also made by Phelan.[17] The latter wishes that Zea would tell us how Mexicans of different social classes function in society, how the individual interacts with his group, how one group relates to another, whether there is any upward mobility, and how much. As pointed out in Chapter Two above, Mexican sociologists have increasingly begun to deal with these problems.[18]

All of these critical observations point to the fact that in contrast to the historiography developed in the United States, which distinguishes clearly between history and philosophy, Mexican historians are quite often philosophers. Since the reverse is similarly true, philosophic concern with the nature of reality results in a merger of history and philosophy. The result is the philosophy of history or the history of ideas.[19]

Zea's writings on Positivism appeared in the early 1940s, the decade which witnessed the formation of a philosophic group calling itself *Hyperión*.[20] The core of its activities centered about the existentialist exploration and attempted definition of the nature of the Mexican ethos. Zea's work was, therefore, in consonance with the intellectual climate of the period—an attempt to capture through history the reality of the Mexican.

Influenced by Ortega and Croce, Zea affirms his fundamental postulates on which is structured his monumental work on Positivism, namely, that: (1) without some basic element or concept, history would be impossible; and (2) philosophy, similarly, is incapable of being forged in the absence of an "intuitive, historical element."[21]

In other words, each history has its own philosophy, its own conceptual scheme, and conversely, each philosophy has a history, i.e., a reality which is peculiar unto itself. Historical interpretation is essential to an understanding of the causes underlying the formation of philosophical conceptions.

Since individual man forms concepts as a result of the thought process—and this, due to confrontation with his circumstance—it follows that philosophy is not eternally universal but is, instead, an expres-

[17] John Leddy Phelan, "México y lo mexicano," *The Hispanic American Historical Review* 36, no. 3 (August 1956), 309-18.
[18] See, for example: Bermúdez (see footnote 6 of Chapter Two), Iturriaga (see footnote 13 of Chapter Two); also Rodolfo Stavenhagen, *Las clases sociales en las sociedades agrarias* (Mexico: Siglo XXI, 1969).
[19] Merrill Rippy, "Theory of History: Twelve Mexicans," *The Americas* 17, no. 3 (January 1961), 223-29.
[20] In Greek mythology, Hyperion was the son of the Earth and Sky, thus symbolizing the concrete and the universal—the chief concern of the study group.
[21] Leopoldo Zea, *El positivismo en México—nacimiento, apogeo y decadencia* (Mexico: Fondo de Cultura Económica, 1968), p. 21.

sion of an individual culture. Zea's method of interpreting philosophy as a means of understanding man is thus historical. The attempt by any given philosophy to claim for itself an exclusive monopoly of the entire realm of truth, and therefore a capability of solving all and sundry problems, has given rise to a series of philosophical contradictions. But these contradictions, maintains Zea, are only apparent; they are, rather, different solutions, offered within the context of diverse circumstances (p. 23). So-called contradictions are simply the results of differing stages of cultural development, easily explained by the historicist approach. In this respect, Zea appears to be strongly influenced by the thinking of Scheler and Mannheim. Ideas and concepts are utilized by social classes to protect and advance their own interests.[22] It is within this context, then, that Zea explains the history of Positivism, not only of Mexico, but in all of Latin America.

This approach is criticized vigorously by Raat, who feels that Zea tends to erect "an overlying pattern in history to which particular events conformed."[23] Such a conceptual scheme runs the risk of acquiring the status of an objective archetype which might condition subsequent research. Certainly, such "fuzzy" expressions as the "Mexican mind" or the "Spirit of the Age" do not approximate the hoped-for objectivity, essential from an historical point of view.[24]

Zea's major concern, namely, how to modernize Latin America without sacrificing her cultural identity, has made him vulnerable on still another count. According to Hale, it is impossible to separate the philosopher from the historian in Zea. When are facts presented as such, asks this critic, and when are they merely interpretations? Good philosophical interpretations may be bad historiography. Hale suggests that the non-Latin American who is not so emotionally involved may be more objective in his treatment of the subject and be able to deal with it in critical fashion with a greater degree of facility. Such comparative studies can transcend the "sterile debate" concerning originality versus imitation in Latin American thought—a theme which appears to have obsessed Zea and his generation.[25] Furthermore, Zea's histories of Positivism suffer from a species of "futurism," i.e., speculative projections toward the future.[26] In a way, it would seem that Zea cannot extricate himself from this difficulty. Writing within the existentialist framework, he realizes that man is not only what he has been,

[22] "... [I]n the past as well as in the present, the dominant modes of thought are supplanted by new categories when the social basis of the group of which these thought-forms are characteristic, disintegrates or is transformed under the impact of social change." Karl Mannheim, *Ideology and Utopia* (New York: Harcourt, Brace and Co., 1946), pp. 73-74.

[23] Raat, p. 13.

[24] Ibid.

[25] Charles A. Hale, "Substancia y método en el pensamiento de Leopoldo Zea," *Historia Mexicana* 20, no. 2 (October-December 1972), 304.

[26] Raat, p. 16.

but also what he may become. Man has to choose between alternatives in the course of his everyday existence—choices which are usually conditioned by the nature of past events as well as by the concrete circumstances of the present. The historian must, therefore, illustrate how the past conditions the range of alternatives for future behaviour. The historian, too, is his own point of departure, a product of his culture, and must act as a "cultural psychoanalyst."[27] As such, he must investigate the origins and trace the development of the various factors which have led, in the case of Mexico, to a so-called inferiority complex. Hopefully, as a result, the Mexican of the future will be released from these subconscious negative elements which have served as obstacles in the path of his mature self-expression. It is in this context that one must evaluate Zea's discussion of the Latin American scene.[28]

C. *The Historicist Perspective*

Every people has something to contribute to world culture. The universal quality of this contribution is measured by the capacity of different groups of people to make themselves understood and to understand others. The circumstantial quality of each contribution should make for a feeling of serenity within the Mexican and serve to integrate him into the world of man. He no longer needs to apologize

[27] Phelan, p. 315.

[28] In a recent publication, *Dependencia y liberación en la cultura latinamericana*, ed. Joaquín Mortiz (Mexico, 1974), Zea replies to the criticism made by Hale and Raat, the two American historians, referred to above. They claim, as has already been suggested, that Zea's excursions into history are slanted by his philosophical predilections and, therefore, make impossible any sort of objective treatment of historical events. The historian or philosopher should not be committed in any way, lest he reveal his bias. According to Raat, Zea's subjectivity invites criticism, since it is difficult to distinguish between history as such and his concerns with both the present and future of Mexico (Raat, p. 15). Moreover, for Zea, the task of philosophy is to alleviate, if not resolve, the problems arising out of the spiritual crisis experienced at present by Western culture. This approach, complains Raat, may be morally praiseworthy, but historically untenable. Historiography requires that the biases of the present be avoided.

But this argument operates in reverse as well, counters Zea. No one works in a vacuum. Foreign critics, as well, cannot escape the charge of subjectivity. They, too, have their bias. Their very criticism reveals an attitude which is the expression of a definite ideology. Raat and Hale are citizens of a powerful nation which utilizes and exploits other less powerful national groups. Their objections should be viewed within the context of their own historical situation. Zea might have added that they belong to a society which is either unable or unwilling to recognize the urges and aspirations of these dependent nations. It is, perhaps, easier under such conditions to be less "subjective."

As though to further justify and reinforce his position, Zea calls upon his old friend and teacher, José Gaos. The latter is quoted in order to show that Zea's contribution to the history of ideas has been valid and desirable. Gaos refers to the central theme found in Zea's numerous works: that of demonstrating the centuries-old imperative on the part of Latin America to achieve cultural emancipation. This is a task which, of necessity, involves Zea in the dissection of the continent's past in order to point the way to a more hopeful and authentic future. The question of subjectivity in these circumstances can no longer be considered of primary importance.

for his presence, or for that matter, his existence. It is now the turn of Mexican philosophers to evaluate and resolve the problems which face them. In the performance of this task it must be remembered that one can no longer speak of Man as a universal entity. Contemporary philosophy challenges the traditional idea of man, considered as unchangeable essence or substance. Man does not possess a determined, definite nature. He is not something already made, but rather a phenomenon which is in the process of making itself, subject to the influences exerted by space and time.

The Mexican, then, is viewed as a man within a specific situation—one which defines and concretizes him. Hitherto the European has been the model upon which the human configuration has been based. But there are other nuances. The European can no longer monopolize human experience. The Mexican, too—and the Latin American in general—possesses experiences, as a result of which he has developed human aspects which, perhaps, have not yet been treated by any philosophy.[29] It is not a question, then, of delving into the Mexican essence, and making that a goal in itself. Instead, Mexican essence is a point of departure to focus upon; it is the essence of man expressed in yet another circumstance, one that is still to be known.

Why speak of the Mexican's essence as a philosophic problem in the first place? After all, Plato, Descartes, Hume, and Kant never inquired into the "essence," the humanity of the Greek, the Frenchman, the Englishman or the German. The reason—and Zea emphasizes this repeatedly—is that Western philosophy has always spoken about man in general. This philosophy was "authentic" because the European was looked upon as Universal Man. Nationality was accidental. The European concrete experience was assumed to be universal and applicable to all of humanity. Anything that did not seem to fit or apply was simply excluded from the concept. "Indigenous" peoples, for example, were considered "marginal" and outside the sphere of civilization. Asia, Africa, Oceania, and finally America, were fit only to be dominated politically and economically. Culturally, they were excluded. Colonial peoples had been exploited materially and had to fight for the preservation of their cultural heritage.

The Spanish Conquest of the New World illustrates this fact more than adequately. The inability of the conqueror to fit the native into the pre-established categories of human beings prompted him to deny human qualities to the Indian. The efforts by Ginés de Sepúlveda, based on Aristotle's philosophy, to prove that the Indian was a slave "by nature," that he was not a rational being, constitute vivid testimony as to the prevailing attitudes of the period, held by outstanding spokesmen for European culture.

[29] *Conciencia y posibilidad del mexicano*, p. 22.

Zea delves into colonial history to give additional weight to his perspectivist approach. The inhabitant of the New World was considered a beast of burden by the Spaniard. Indian culture was the work of the Devil; the Conqueror could therefore justify his social, political, and economic domination. God had made the discovery of America possible because it had to be brought under the influence of the Western World. But history plays its ironic tricks. Eventually the Indian would influence the Conqueror. Although the Spaniard would soon feel that he was no longer European, he did not quite know how to be a Mexican. The native Indian culture did not disappear in spite of the fact that Europeans had come to Christianize and "civilize." The European soon came under the spell of the native ambience. He was not so sure that he had "civilized" the Indian. The world of the latter, apparently eliminated—or so it was thought—soon emerged. Even though the Spaniard had built churches on the foundations of native temples, his version of Christianity was soon "tainted" by Indian beliefs and deities. And just as Greece "took captive her Roman Conquerors," the New World vanquished those who had come to "colonize" its inhabitants. The *criollo* was now caught between two cultures. He no longer felt himself part of Europe, that "universal" world par excellence. He now felt left out and inferior to the culture he was trying to emulate.[30] Ironically enough, the *criollo* exhibited the same behaviour patterns vis-à-vis other social groups of the American-born social hierarchy (e.g. the *mestizos*) as the *peninsular* had evinced toward him.

The first stumbling block, as mentioned, in the way of recognizing the essential humanity of the Indian was located in the theological realm. In fact, Mexican philosophy can be said to have begun with an inquiry into the nature of the Indian. Sepúlveda's opponent, Bartolomé de las Casas, defended the Indian's humanity by pointing to the similarities shared by both the Conquerors and the vanquished.

The second obstacle indicated by Zea was scientific in nature. By now Zea has enlarged his canvas. He is no longer referring exclusively to the Mexican scene. His meditations carry him along new pathways to include the entire continent in his view of humanism. In the eyes of Europe the inhabitant of the New World leads a substandard existence. In the name of European science, Latin America is labelled "inferior." It is a subcontinent, inhabited by subhumans, by "animals of the first order," claims Buffon, the French naturalist.[31] The Prussian naturalist, De Pauw, labels Americans "children" who have not yet attained their full humanity. They are "stupid, incurably lazy, and incapable of any progress" (p. 23). Inferiority is no longer the result of some sin or fall from grace, as was the judgment of the Spanish missionaries, but a result of racial and physical causes which the victim is incapable of

[30] *America como conciencia* (Mexico: Cuadernos Americanos, 1953), p. 103.
[31] *El Occidente y la conciencia de México* (Mexico: Porrúa y Obregón, 1953), p. 22.

changing—a verdict rendered by a "scientific" West which has by now become de-Christianized, and which justifies its subjugation of non-Western peoples in the name of technical progress. In short, civilizing these "backward" nations is possible, but only at the hands of the Western World—a discrimination which in the case of Mexico results in self-deprecation.

The Latin American continent is also attacked from the philosophical point of view. Hegel had written that America was incapable of creativity, that it could only imitate and had not done anything for universal culture, i.e., Western culture. If the essence of man is history, Americans have not yet made universal history, and were therefore lacking in human dimensions (p. 31).

Yet historicism, it seems, may also act as a boomerang. Its arguments may prove counterproductive. For it also stimulates so-called "marginal" people to investigate their past. These also make history even though it may not be the Western brand. Quoting Arnold Toynbee in this connection, Zea suggests that Western civilization is based on an egocentric illusion. Within the Western frame of reference the nonutilization of technical knowledge is interpreted as a sign of inferiority. To civilize is to "technify." Those who dominate technology have set themselves up to control the world. Yet to civilize also means to humanize. The West has been forced to pause as it becomes aware of the dehumanizing effects of technology. One would infer that it is now the turn of the "marginal" countries to "humanize" and "re-educate" the technological "masters." Behold the paradox: the product is "civilizing" the producer (pp. 35-36)!

* * * * *

Zea's vigorous criticism of Latin America's attempts to amputate her "barbaric" past in an attempt to become "civilized," instead of assimilating and rising above it to achieve a synthesis between past and present, has led him to meditate upon the relationship that exists between the continent and other countries of the Third World. He sees many possibilities for Latin America in this connection. For example, the Third World can profit from the experience of Latin America, especially since the latter has already "enjoyed" the benefits of contact with the "civilizations" of the West, e.g., the American model to the north. There is one important difference, he is quick to point out ironically. Latin America is even worse off than Asia or Africa. The latter continents were isolated by the European because they were considered "sub-human"; they did not resemble the Europeans at all. Latin America, by contrast, is European, in origin at least, but has sunk to a subhuman level.[32]

[32] *La filosofía americana como filosofía sin más* (Mexico: Siglo XXI, Editores, S.A., 1969), p. 19.

Zea reviews the history of Latin America's attempts to rid itself of its "barbarism," beginning with the colonial period and ending with the Mexican Revolution of 1910. The Spanish missionaries had defended the "marginal groups of history" in terms of their concept of Man as a religious and philosophical archetype. Subsequently, the archetypes evolved into "progress" and "technology," also European models to be imitated, in the process of which the indigenous population was looked upon as a means to be utilized or destroyed.

Spain's policies resulted initially in the creation of a proletariat consisting of Indians, and subsequently, mestizos. In the decades following Independence, an influx of European immigrants added further to the variety of the ethnic composition of the continent. In any case, the European archetype was always present. The Latin American added, superimposed, and copied, but never quite absorbed the foreign model. The result was a collection of beautiful constitutions, utopias, republican patterns of government, in countries which had not yet surmounted and assimilated Spanish despotism (p. 21). Civil wars were fought between those who wished to uproot the Spanish past and those who resisted foreign importations. The latter were ideas and institutions which were far from being an outgrowth of the Latin American past; in short, wars involving dual utopias—the past and the future! Even those romantics who spoke in terms of creating an authentic, national culture were themselves inspired by the archetypal Europe.

The history of the continent since Independence may be viewed as a series of oscillations from one extreme to another. Action provoked reaction. Imitation of foreign models led to an affirmation of "nativist" values. Nativism, in turn, called forth an aspiration toward universality.

After 1810, the mestizos and Indians of Mexico were greatly disappointed. Only the *criollos* had reaped the fruits of Independence. Eventually, the fermentation concerning the "mental emancipation of America" which the romantics had proclaimed was to lead to the formation of a mestizo bourgeoisie, similar to the European and North American archetypes. There were those who resisted Mexico's attempts to enter the material world of the West. The Revolution of 1857, the *Reforma*, was the "response" to that "challenge." Nevertheless, the Mexican bourgeoisie utilized Comtian and later Spencerian Positivist doctrines—more imitation!—to advance their social and economic interests. Again, it was a case of a poor copy. The Mexicans attempted to imitate the European bourgeoisie, but ended by serving it in a subsidiary role. The result? More alienation.

The Uruguayan, Rodó, in Toynbee's terms, was also a "response," a reaction against the excessive emphasis on material values engendered by Positivism in Latin America. So were Caso and Vasconcelos in Mexico, Korn in Argentina, Deustua in Peru, and Molina in Chile. Zea makes the point that in all of these cases the pendulum swung away from the archetype of materialism and pragmatism, and in the direction of seeking and finding Man within each man, as part of the quest of identity. The final stage, in the case of Mexico, was the Revolution of 1910. It is here that one could perceive overtones of a new cultural nationalism that transcended colonialism and underdevelopment. But the Revolution was not to lead to an exaggerated nationalism. It was merely a longed-for stage in the cultural development of the Mexican, a catalyst designed to make him pause and ask: What is my position as a man among men?

At this point Zea establishes a connection with the Third World. The West has long dominated Asia and Africa. Yet, curiously enough, Western philosophy has itself provided the necessary elements whereby those who are alienated can rid themselves of their alienation by means of a proper utilization of these very same elements. The Asians and the Africans, like the Latin Americans, want to know what their position is in this Western-dominated world. Hence, the questions posed are similar.

Zea insists that an application of the Hegelian dialectic will solve the problem of identity in all cases. The formula is well known: to be what one is means to know what one has been in order not to have to continue being it. Each stage includes within itself the stages which have preceded it, and in turn leads the way to new solutions. This is what reality continues to require of each culture and this is essentially what philosophy has been all along in the Old World. The process was subsequently duplicated in the New World: Scholasticism, Enlightenment, Romanticism, Jacobinism, Positivism, Creative freedom, historicism, and existentialism.

Yet the duplication has not always been exact. There have been exceptions. For example, the Mexican Revolution, in contrast to the French and Russian, did not seek solutions to problems on a world scale, such as the well-being of an abstract humanity. It sought only to solve concrete problems. An interesting contrast is developed by Zea. The bases for the other revolutions, namely the French and the Russian, were laid by philosophical theory (e.g., the philosophy of Progress and Enlightenment, and of Dialectical Materialism). Such was not the case in Mexico which, Zea hastens to add, does not imply an absence of ideals.[33] The Mexican Revolution was participated in by men of all classes, holding diverse ideologies. But the ideologies arose out of the Revolution and crystallized, so to speak, as a result. The Revolution was not prepared by these men; it prepared them (pp. 28-29). All theories which had attempted to interpret the Mexican Revolution were discarded; they were inadequate in their explanations of Mexican reality. The Revolution was not influenced by foreign, "imported doctrines."

---

[33] *Conciencia y posibilidad*, p. 25.

It was national in scope, and represented an upsurge of national feeling, the result, apparently, of a turning inward upon itself by the nation as a whole. It was the rebellion of the dispossessed, and in large measure, of the Indian who represented the nation. It was expressed in painting, literature, archaeology, and finally, in philosophy (p. 31). Mexico had at long last taken the first step to dissociate itself from foreign models and borrowed formulas—the result of a desire to take stock of itself. The Revolution was thus the most effective means of crystallizing national values whereby the country could earn a place in the "universal" sun; a reaction of man in a specific circumstance, revealing his "profile" which had been submerged for centuries.

* * * * *

Taking stock of oneself means becoming aware of one's limitations; it involves a realization that these limitations are obstacles that lie in the way of arriving at universal truths. It is not enough to strive to arrive at a Latin American truth. Of greater importance is the effort to reach a truth valid for all men, even though this may be unattainable. Zea attempts all along to achieve a happy synthesis of two philosophic orientations: one road, which leads to universality; the other, more limited, which deals with historical, sociological and psychological facets of the problem. Mexican philosophical studies have tended to deal in greater measure with the latter category. Zea has felt all along that Mexicans have for too long meditated upon the meditations of others.[34] We do not wish to be rationalists or existentialists, he asserts, merely because these happen to be the fashion. We will be so, however, if they furnish us with the elements for possible solutions to our own problems (p. 16).

Zea returns to the notion of Mexican "inadequacy." This has its origin in the fear of being a reflection of other cultures, a fear which is characteristic of colonial peoples, including Mexicans. The European is confident that his culture has universal dimensions. The Mexican, and by extension, the Latin American, is convinced that his culture is inadequate. "Europe creates and re-creates its classics; we ignore ours" (p. 18). This is so simply because the Mexican believes that his classics are not similar to those of Europe. Zea argues that it is the Mexican's perspective that makes his thoughts *different*, but not inadequate.

Europe's "universalism"—itself an outgrowth of local perspectives—has excluded other cultural currents which do not adapt to its point of view. Mexican "insufficiency" does not have to be negative in its implications. It is simply the result of a realization of the immensity of the task which still lies ahead and of that which still has to be assimilated before the Mexican can approach anything resembling

---

[34] *América como conciencia*, p. 14.

an authentic universal culture. In the process, he should avoid the pitfalls of a false nationalism, equally insufficient; instead, the road to universality should be traversed via his own reality. It is this reality which affords him the security of what has already been created; the quest itself, the search for universality, should yield a sense of "creative insecurity" (pp. 20-21).

An understanding of past history—of events and their motivations—will make for a greater philosophical awareness of what it is that makes us Mexicans, Peruvians, Argentinians, etc., and in addition, Spanish Americans. The past, then, once assimilated, will no longer represent a threat to our future (pp. 24-25). This becomes the legitimate area of study for the history of ideas, an area, unfortunately, which seems to frustrate Zea; for it is neither history nor philosophy. According to him, scholars in this field have always been in a dilemma. They have been criticized by historians for being too abstract, and by philosophers who have accused them of being excessively concrete (p. 26).

In *América en la historia*,[35] Zea has amplified his dimensions, proceeding not only from Mexico to Latin America as a whole—which we find in embryonic form in his earlier works—but also from Latin America to Europe. The enlarged canvas includes, more specifically, the historical division within Europe itself, which dates from the Reformation, and the repercussions thereof experienced in the New World, i.e., the two Americas. This perspective, according to Zea, would explain the original "marginality" of the Iberian peninsula vis-à-vis the remainder of western Europe; the split between Catholicism and the "modern age," the latter represented by England, France, and Holland—a division which was to plague the Latin American psyche in the centuries which followed.

We are thus brought face to face with the relationship which Latin America bears to the so-called "main" stream of history. The crisis of European civilization was brought about by the Reformation, and was due in large measure to the failure on the part of Erasmus to reconcile the existing conflicts. The result was the emergence of the "modern" nations, in contrast to Spain and Portugal. The latter assumed a defensive posture and attempted to maintain the older status quo.

In his earlier works Zea had advanced the belief that modern man, having lost his faith in the old Christian world, sought a framework wherein to locate his new ideals. The new, "modern" nations were opposed to the Church and feudalism. What the "new European" could not realize in Europe he would attempt in America. In fact, Descartes' "modern man" saw in America the ideal site for the realization of his fantasies. America was the land which had had nothing to do

---

[35] (Mexico: Fondo de Cultura Económica, 1957.)

with Europe's past—a past from which modern man sought escape.[36] America, then, was the dream of the Renaissance man, the land of promise, the pilot study for what Europe would become some day. The modern era, ushered in by the Reformation, was characterized by freedom of the individual. He was now the centre of the universe; he was answerable to himself alone, not to traditional social pressures or divine powers. Quoting Hegel, Zea sums it all up: America was "a country for those who were fed up with the historical museum of the Old World" (p. 81).

In the schism which occurred in European Christendom "modern" man was identified with Protestantism. North America adopted this spirit of European culture and made it its own in the course of its development. This was not the case with Latin America. Its spirit was that of the Iberian peninsula which had been "left behind." The conflict between the two "spirits" was essentially what lay at the root of Latin America's tragic dilemma. Unlike its neighbour to the north, Latin America, in attempting to accept the patterns of "modern Europe" and assimilate Western values, went counter to the cultural spirit in which it had been reared. In the conflict between Catholicism and Modernism, accepting one set of values, regrettably enough, implied rejecting the other (not only the spirit, but also the fruits). Some Latin Americans had thought that by adopting the fruits as well as the procedures of "modern" Europe, the spirit would follow; for example, that the adoption of a constitution modelled upon that of the United States would lead to a liberal democracy, or that the development of free trade and economic competition would result in a healthy capitalism. However, events and traditions, part and parcel of the "marginal" Iberian heritage, were to prove otherwise.

Zea engages in a detailed analysis of the differences between the two Americas against the European background of Catholicism versus Modernism, an analysis which he continues in many articles published subsequently. Whereas the North American pioneers sought to realize the utopias dreamed of by More, Bacon, and Campanella, the Latin American colonists merely intended to transfer and perpetuate the world of Spain and Portugal to the new continent. The North Americans severed their connections with the old societies of feudal origin. They set out to conquer virgin territory and create a new world in accordance with the precepts of modernity. On the other hand, the Latin Americans did not burn their bridges behind them. They sought to reproduce an old world instead of creating a new one, in the hope of gaining privileges they did not enjoy in the old country.

The Anglo-American did not want to have anything to do with his past. He was an "innocent," starting out anew.[37] The Latin American,

---

[36] *América como conciencia*, p. 69.
[37] *América en la historia*, p. 23.

by contrast, sought to make out of America another Christian Europe, only to discover that Europe had already embarked upon new paths. His subsequent frustration was the result of a guilt feeling; he was not able to reproduce his model, and therefore he blamed the "primitive" American scene for his failure. He had, in short, inherited a culture, apparently "out of season." He, too, had wanted, like the Anglo-American, to be an "innocent," to start with a *tabula rasa*, so to speak. But unlike "modern" man, he felt weighed down by his past, his sense of guilt, his "original sin" (p. 26). His past was a limitation, instead of a point of departure. What the Latin American failed to see was that this past was not merely an obstacle to be eliminated, but that it continued to be an integral part of the present, and was also a function of the future.

The basic problem—and here Zea seems to be complaining—is that history has up to this point been forged by the West, and the West has cast aside the Iberian peninsula, regarding it as of no importance. However, other nations—non-Western—such as India and China, have also succeeded in making history. Or else, like Africa, they will do so in the future. In this sense, Latin America is similar to the latter group. Both past and future meet in Latin America, but the linkage to establish the present is missing. From the Western point of view—a somewhat arrogant one—Latin America is nothing; it is form without content, unless, of course, it becomes part of the West and adopts its values.

But Zea protests: Latin America's history is also Western, although not in the same form as that of the dominant "modern" West. It is the history of man in certain circumstances—neither inferior nor superior. This lack of historical awareness has caused the Latin American to accept his position of marginality vis-à-vis the West. But he is certainly not marginal in his own concrete condition. That is why Zea urges him to develop the capacity to bestow a universal quality upon his original-ity, i.e., a universality which would be equally valid for others in a similar situation. This is certainly a more desirable development than what has happened thus far: the West "universalized" other peoples by bringing their values to them, despite the fact that the historical situa-tion of the latter was not similar to the European circumstance (pp. 31-32).

After all, the Iberian world also had its "modernists," both in Spain and Latin America. The Erasmists, Feijoo, the eighteenth-century "eclectics," Bolívar, Hidalgo, the Krausists—these are but a few who tried to "modernize" while retaining older values. There is no reason why Latin America should not enjoy the individual dignity and com-forts made possible by the "modern" West. The trouble is that this "modern" spirit has degenerated into a glorified individualism and a rampant dehumanization which have justified aggression against other peoples of the world. Ruthless, inhumane behaviour in the name of "civilization" and "progress": this is Zea's main thesis, one which, as time goes on, will induce him to stress in increasing fashion, the identity of interests between Latin America and the countries of the Third World. The refrain is familiar: those in the Western World who have for centuries spoken of dignity and happiness were the first to deny these to peoples in other parts of the globe, simply because advocating or granting these rights to others would have meant a reduction in their own comforts and privileges (p. 35).

* * * * *

Zea as a philosopher of history believes there is a pattern to be observed in the development of the West. The values of "modern" civilization are for him political democracy and the creation of wealth—both the results of man's efforts. Man, in fact, is himself historical, since, in the words of Ortega, he "makes himself." He therefore does not accept the past in which he has had no share. The past is simply a rung in the ladder of the future. It is something that was, but does not have to keep on being, since it must make room for the "new" man, the "new" culture to be formed. In the Western view, the past must be overcome in order to build the culture of the future. History thus becomes an instrumentality with which to justify the future (p. 43). This means that modern man will use the so-called "world of nature" as a point of departure to make a "world of culture." In making his own history, he assumes responsibility for what *he* will do, not for what others have done before him. Implicit in these assumptions is the idea of progress, attainable for *all* men. Western culture stresses this central fact: all men should have the same opportunities; all are equal. Personal effort and individual capacity will tell the story. This will, of course, lead to a justification of future inequities and privileges; the latter are not inherited, but acquired. Succeeding generations never begin anew, as did the pioneers. The descendants are supposed to continue from the point at which their ancestors stopped (p. 72).

In the Western view, then, progress is equal to accumulation and investment. What is accumulated in one generation becomes the point of departure for more accumulation by the next. Individual accumulation thus leads to group accumulation, giving rise to the emergence of social classes. The capacity of the individual subsequently determines his continued membership in a particular class which, in turn, conditions his further accumulation of wealth, over and above his personal needs. He thus becomes an instrument of an entity which has by now transcended and gone beyond him. In short, what he had contributed to and moulded originally, now controls him.

Man dies, but the fruits of his labour remain and thus become immortalized. God can therefore be said to justify the domination by those who work over those who do not—a central expression of the Calvinist ethic. Since this also represents the triumph of good over evil, it follows that modern, Western man is predestined to triumph over those who will not submit to his governance voluntarily.

Zea expresses repeatedly his concern with this phase of Western history: the Calvinist ethic as manifested in the New World, especially in contrast to the development of the Latin American ethos. The modern *Weltanschauung* of the Western World, which begins in the sixteenth century, has its roots in the Christian culture and the classical period, true enough, but denies its connections with them. Zea maintains that not only does the West reject and displace its own past, but also that of other cultures with which it has come in contact. Its philosophers and historians justify expansion and domination within the framework of the doctrine of indefinite progress; these also seek to insure that the West not be displaced in the way it has displaced those which have existed before it, i.e., all non-European countries (p. 59).

Zea shuttles continually from the modern European scene to the New World—north and south—comparing the two Americas, and then back again, from Latin America to the rest of the world, including Asia and Africa, in an effort to focus properly upon his main concern—the Latin American perspective. And throughout the entire process he strives to capture the so-called "flavour" or "profile" of a given culture, which enables one to speak of the "spirit" of a people, as contrasted with that of other ethnic groups. In this sense it becomes possible to fashion a history of ideas or a philosophy of history, since these involve interpretation and the search for meaning. This can be achieved by delving into the past in an attempt to explain people and circumstances in order to implement more effectively plans for the future, while bearing in mind that these very same plans condition the explanation of the events of the past. "Each age has its own interpretation of history in accordance with its present and future interests."[38]

The profile of America can, therefore, never be considered *in vacuo*, divorced from sources which gave it its origin. In this case, one must hearken back to the two contending forces which were locked in battle in early sixteenth-century Europe. For the American, historical awareness was influenced by these two ideological enemies which Zea speaks of: A Christian or Catholic interpretation of America, as opposed to the "modern" interpretation. In either case, both the inhabitant of the New World and his concrete circumstance were subordinate to the European.[39]

The main problem, then—an old one with Zea, but now reformulated—is the position of Latin American culture within the

---

[38] "El puritanismo en la conciencia norteamericana," in *America en la conciencia de Europa* (Mexico: Los Presentes, 1955), pp. 82-83.

[39] See pp. 73-74.

context of universal culture. It is impossible to grasp the essence of America from the Latin American point of view if one does not understand the nature of the Anglo-American perspective.

These two diverse cultural currents were transplanted from Europe to America. In the case of Latin America, what was involved was an extension of Christianity's orbit to the New World as the Iberian peninsula understood the term. In the case of the United States, it was a question of modifying old Christian values or even creating new ones. The first orientation was forced to retreat and to take refuge behind Spain's territorial frontiers; the second perspective expanded throughout the rest of Europe as well as North America.

It has already been pointed out that this latter perspective, "modernism," as distinct from traditional Catholicism, made possible the vast expansion and influence of the Western World. Latin America was aware of this development, but found itself at a disadvantage, because its origin was derived from the ideology of the "losing" contender. It could not emulate the "winner," although it made some efforts to do so, because its cultural heritage stood in the way. But there was also another obstacle. Latin America saw itself as merely a means to be exploited by the West in its expansionist drive. It was no longer a question of Christianity versus Modernism—especially in the present century—but rather between the United States, the undisputed leader of the modern world, and a group of nations which aspired to be an active part of that same world.[40]

The United States, and the Western World in general, had assigned to Latin America a role similar to the one played by Asia, Africa, and Oceania. But then Latin America was not content to be relegated to that position; it insisted on being part of the world which it had been attempting to imitate, a world which had served as a model.

The emergent conflicts, then, were not only the result of a clash between two conceptions, but also an outgrowth of the reluctance on the part of the leaders of this expansionist movement to make room for others. Christianity, as interpreted by the expansionist West, did not include everybody in the category of humanity. Zea labels this outright treason; the West was guilty of betrayal of its own theoretical principles.

Zea makes the point repeatedly: European philosophers—classical, medieval, and modern—had never concerned themselves with the specific, since they assumed their culture and the individuals who created it to be universal. It is only in recent years, due to a series of crises, that European philosophy has turned its attention to the concrete and individual. The "accidental" quality of one's being is now recognized. The Latin American has long experienced this accidental quality; he has never felt "universal." In fact, he has always wanted to be

---

[40] *La esencia de lo americano* (Burenos Aires: Editorial Pleamar, 1971), p. 12.

part of the universal stream—a goal he could achieve only by recognizing the nature of his humanity in a concrete situation—by sharing
common problems with others.

The concrete, then, far from impeding a realization of what is
human, advances the quality of humanity, gives it impetus, makes it
more real, and universalizes it—a universalism not granted by European culture to non-Europeans. Paradoxically, the European now
finds himself in a position similar to that experienced by Latin America
for some time: an awareness of his "circumstantiality," his "accidence";
he has, in short, not been as universal as he had supposed. In fact, he
has all along been quite provincial (pp. 16-17). The Latin American, by
contrast, has felt his "circumstance" since the discovery of the New
World. His problem has been his awareness that his existence is marginal. His very awareness can be said to have been imposed upon him
by so-called "universal" European thought (pp. 19-20).

North American colonization, in contrast to that of the Iberian
portion of the hemisphere, was the reflection of the "modern" European spirit which had broken with the old "establishment" of the
Middle Ages. The new social class, the bourgeoisie, opposed to the
Church and the nobility, believed in personal effort. Each man was the
author of his own works.[41] Subsequent differences were therefore
justified on natural grounds. The accumulation of goods determined
the formation of the new social class and spelled progress—the deifica-
tion of man's productivity. The new social condition was given tran-
scendental meaning and justification.

What is important in this development is a shift of emphasis: from
an external determinism, i.e., man's behaviour as conditioned by outer
forces, to one which originates within himself. It is no longer God or an
Absolute Spirit which decides, but rather a substance whose existence
depends on man's will power. Divinity exists because man endows it
with a sense of being as a result of his labour. In this respect, God
becomes dependent upon man; He is created by man, an expression of
his power. God is pure human possibility—the ever-present goal toward which man aspires in order to justify his existence.[42]

Modern man, in short, conceives of his actions as being those of
God; he is an instrument of progress. In this examination of the
Puritan ethic, Zea is preparing the way for a critical analysis of the
policies of the United States vis-à-vis Latin America. Since the new
socioeconomic class considers its actions identical with those of the
Divine, all other social groups whose interests do not coincide or which
clash with its own, will have to be dominated or eliminated. This new
perspective now represents the thinking of Western culture, and is
reflected in the theocratic order of colonial New England. Anything

[41] See pp. 75-76.
[42] "El Puritanismo," p. 93.

else is an expression of evil, barbarism and irrationality. Corrective measures taken against these manifestations are justified in the name of God and Progress. Good has to triumph over Evil (p. 97).

In the Puritan ethic work evolves into an end in itself, since it is not deemed sufficient to work merely to earn in order to provide for the bare necessities of life. In view of the direct relationship between God and the individual, and the salvation of man by his own efforts—both premises posited by Calvinism—work for the greater glory of God results in greater profit for the individual who accumulates wealth. Property in this world thus becomes an index of the possibility of salvation in the other. He who succeeds in a material sense is more than just a man; he is God's instrument. God speaks through his works.

The Calvinist belief applied to the American scene coloured the Puritan's attitude toward the Indian. Unlike the "new" European, the North American native worked only to satisfy his immediate necessities. "To save for a rainy day" was alien to him. Since he did not save, he had nothing to invest. In the Calvinist view, he hadn't lived up to his mission, and consequently, had to be rescued from the devil. The Spaniard attempted to "incorporate" the native into the Catholic world. The Puritan also believed that his mission was to spread Christianity. But with this very important difference: he preached the gospel in order to offer the Indians the opportunity to save themselves. However, not all who had this opportunity would be saved. This was reserved only for those who were predestined to receive the "call" from God. The Puritans, therefore, could not "incorporate" the Indian, since receiving grace was linked with material success, a difficult feat for the native who was faced with a handicap to begin with—that of having been conquered by the colonizers (pp. 111-12). Even if one were to accept the good intentions of the Puritans, it was inconceivable that the native could bridge the gap between his own form of social organization and that of the Puritan. The Indian had no choice but to resign himself indefinitely, without too great a possibility of saving his soul. Or else, he could return to his "natural" world. In any case, this constituted sufficient proof in the eyes of the Puritan that the native had not been "called," demonstrating thereby his low state of humanity, and the triumph of the devil. The native was definitely lost; nothing could be done to save him. Only by his own efforts could he save himself. Failure to do so was clear evidence of how far removed he was from God. The Indian thus represented Evil. Fear of contamination resulted in discrimination. It was necessary to isolate him. Social contacts between Indians and Puritans were taboo.

Zea continues to weave his web, placing the Indian within the context of Puritan ideology. Coupled with the above perspective is the belief that God had given this virgin land of the New World to the Puritans in order that they might gather its fruits as a result of their labours. The Indian was regarded as an obstacle since he had never done anything to transform his environment. Within this context it was easy to deprive him of his lands in order to extend the domination of Good over Evil. Expansion was thus justified in the name of religion. All obstacles were regarded as manifestations of the Evil principle. Eventually, within this philosophical framework, the entire Latin American continent came to be viewed as an obstacle. The relations between the two Americas were established. The points of friction, at first religious in origin, and subsequently economic in nature, became crystallized.

* * * * *

The economic implications of Calvinism had their repercussions in the area of political theory. The "modern" bourgeois of the West saw an intimate relationship between individual freedom and liberal democracy, insofar as these were conducive to the development of material comfort and economic expansionism. Those who were not swept up in this current were considered "immature," "backward," or outside the realm of history. Liberal doctrine held that individual ability led to social welfare and national prosperity. Consequently, those who achieved success could not understand the mentality of groups of individuals who were not concerned primarily with material well-being. The latter, therefore, did not deserve any consideration. They were failures because of their incapacity.

The individualistic spirit, characteristic of Protestantism, had exploited Asia and Africa. It had attacked Spain's management of her colonies in the New World. It had even inspired these colonies to fight for and achieve their independence, only to exploit them subsequently in much more effective fashion than Spain had ever done. New-born nations who wanted to enter the contest involving economic advance had to pay a heavy price. The leaders of the West dictated the terms. Any latecomers had to assume a subordinate role.

Thus this Adam Smith type of economic liberalism also extended to nations; it was not applicable to individuals alone. The wealthy utilized science in order to make nature work for man. Unfortunately, it was only the rich who had the means and the time to utilize science in this way. The control of scientific technology led to expansionism and domination. Those in control thought they were doing the "under-developed" peoples a favour by creating opportunities whereby the more capable would triumph. They forgot that it was quite possible that some of these "underdeveloped" areas might have been exposed to another type of cultural conditioning—one which had not prepared them for the market of "free competition."

for someone—these are associated with the personalized "community" idea. However, one cannot agree that these practices do not exist in the "impersonal society" of the United States. If anything, they are probably developed to a greater degree and on a more sophisticated level of efficiency. As far as personal relationships are concerned, it would seem that depersonalization is increasingly a function of highly industrialized social systems; the "family feeling" is more easily evident in less developed societies, technologically speaking. It follows that in certain Latin American countries, where, for example, industrialization has increased, a corresponding degree of "impersonality" has crept in and coexists with older, more traditional attitudes. This is precisely one of the contentions advanced by Zea. Latin America, since Independence, tried to combine two contradictory worlds: one which it had inherited with another it was striving to emulate.

Still another factor deserves to be mentioned in connection with the comparison between the two Americas. In accordance with the spirit of the "new" society, the social organization of the northern colonies had to be forged by means of a Compact to which the individual committed himself in order to attain the peace offered him by security. Society's limits were those imposed by the individual upon himself. Gradually, individual freedom assumed growing importance vis-à-vis the social order, but still within the constraints necessary to preserve that order.

In spite of its rigidity, Calvinism permitted the formation of the first democratic communities in the New World. The theocratic democracy of New England was based on a pact with God, entered into only by a chosen few. As has been pointed out, one of the basic tenets of Puritanism held that it was not enough to contemplate God; one had to glorify Him by working. Diligence, moderation, sobriety, and thrift were not only Christian but also businessmen's virtues. Work and effort were considered proof that salvation had been achieved.[46] The messianic concept of establishing the Kingdom of God here on earth was seen as justification for westward expansion. The Redeemer would liberate unproductive lands and bring civilization to those people who still found themselves beyond the pale of progress.

Democracy, thus conceived, came to be a form of social organization, peculiar to an "elect" or "pre-destined" group of individuals. It was also of divine origin, since God was the personal guarantor. This perspective would ultimately determine the relationship between the United States and other peoples. The latter, if unable to achieve similar democratic institutions, would be looked upon as "incapable," rather than products of a different set of cultural circumstances.

This ideological posture played no small role in the policy developed subsequently by the United States with respect to its dealings

---

[46] "El Puritanismo," p. 126.

with Latin America. Whereas the Puritan paid homage to the cult of work for the sake of work, and therefore considered idleness wicked, the Latin mentality did not convert work into a cult. Consequently, the latter, in the eyes of the Puritan, was incapable of fulfilling man's mission on earth as God had ordained. The Spanish colonies had to be encouraged to rid themselves of this attitude which was an obstacle to democracy. If the Latin American was a product, or perhaps even a victim, of his circumstances, the Puritan, by contrast, considered man as capable of rising above circumstance.

* * * * *

The difficulties experienced by the newly independent Spanish colonies in their attempts to realize democratic forms of government convinced the United States that it was dealing with "marginal" people, as yet unprepared for democracy. In the name of "progress," the United States embarked upon its policy of "Manifest Destiny" and penetrated the lands to the south in an attempt "to compensate for Latin American inferiority" (pp. 133-34).

Zea's entire thesis rests on the belief that Latin America (as well as Asia and Africa) has been exploited by the "modern" nations of the West, particularly the United States in more recent decades. Latin America has been denied opportunities to develop national independence and economic progress. He sees this as a consistent pattern of historical development, making periodic references to Toynbee to prove his point. The latter has stated in a recent article:

> Modern man has been induced to overcome traditional scruples about giving free rein to human greed by a doctrine that has made greed look respectable. It has been asserted that the selfish pursuit of individual or sectional economic advantage is socially beneficial. . . . The unleashing of greed by this doctrine has been the psychological driving force behind the modern way of life in the technologically "developed" countries.[47]

Zea would have all people share in the new universal "modern" civilization. Yet at least one contemporary Latin Americanist has suggested that Zea utilizes particular events to make them conform to and illustrate his theory. Such terms as "liberalism," "imperialism," and "colonialism" are used as though they were unchanging concepts.[48] Certainly Zea appears to be on solid ground when he criticizes the arrogance of the United States vis-à-vis other "less developed" nations. Nevertheless, one may ask with some justification, as does Griffin, whether the so-called "backwardness" attributed to these peoples is due *only* to Western exploitation! Some of the elements which comprise this

[47] Arnold Toynbee, "Making Greed Look Respectable," *The Montreal Star*, January 26, 1974.
[48] Charles C. Griffin, " 'América en la historia' by Leopoldo Zea," *American Historical Review* 58 (April 1958), 709-11.

"underdevelopment" may conceivably be traced to the traditions of these various peoples.

Zea seems to take cognizance of this criticism. He analyzes the role of the mother country, Spain, with respect to the development of the West. Spain, the bulwark of Catholicism, was excluded from the European family of nations, because it remained alien to the dictates of "reason" which ushered in the Modern Age. Spain's mission—the defence of Catholicism—alienated her from the rest of Europe which had made "progress" the all-important watchword. Spain had wanted to join Europe—Zea's contention—but was rejected. She was considered the personification of retrogression and placed outside the march of history by powerful interests, alien to Catholicism, which had taken control of Europe's destiny.

The gap was so wide that Spain even fought against Europeanizing influences within her own borders. Was the West to blame for this? For her shutting herself up behind the Pyrenees? Some elements in Spain, a minority, to be sure, had fought a losing battle in an attempt to reconcile Catholicism and "modernism." Padre Feijoo is a shining example of Spain's attempt to enter the European stream. However, Europe was not disposed to receive her and share its influence with her. On the contrary, Europe preferred to ally itself with feudal and theocratic elements within Spain in order to prevent her from becoming more liberal.[49] For example, after Napoleon's defeat, Spain was to be "westernized," but only on the West's terms, i.e., in a subordinate position. Behold, therefore, this strange alliance against those who would liberalize Spain, an odd couple, indeed: the "modern" forces of the West which did not want to lose its privileges, joined with the internal theocracy of Spain which likewise did not wish to be stripped of its power.

This bizarre union has served to explain the anticlericalism of the liberal, a hostility rooted in his realization of the role played by his country's feudal past and the power exerted by the Catholic Church. But unfortunately the liberal never had any mass support; he was in the minority (like his counterpart in Latin America), since the masses had always been steeped in the past. Oligarchic mentality and Church interests thus joined forces with "progressive" European nations to place Spain in a position of marginality—a development contested continually by a frustrated Spanish liberalism.

The "anti-modern" perspective of Spain can be traced to economic factors. The inhabitants of Castille, the key province in the historical process of Spanish unification, could always live off the land without having to concern themselves with economic pursuits. After immediate needs had been satisfied, all excess energy could be expended more fruitfully in other directions. Since there was no felt need to worry

[49] *América en la historia*, p. 144.

about technology, incapacity in this direction was the inevitable result. But incapacity also led to a contempt for technology, a convenient disguise for a fancied superiority. The Spaniard could only concern himself with the "higher" things in life. He was more interested in achieving immortality through fame and glory, not by means of an accumulation of wealth. Business had a disintegrating effect upon the human personality. Working on the land, by contrast, made the Iberian better suited for noble deeds. (One wonders how much labour was actually performed personally by the Spanish landholder). This romantic conception of the Spanish personality advanced by Zea was transferred to the New World. It contributed to the "marginality" of both the mother country and her colonies at a time when the rest of Europe, spurred on by the Protestant ethic, was more interested in commercial activities. It also produced the well-known syndrome of the "personality" cult, i.e., the exaggerated emphasis upon the value of the person (often to the point of arrogance): a case of men who love their community, but who at the same time look upon themselves as the main ingredient of that community—so much so that they feel they can do without it (pp. 226-27). The end results of this attitude have been weakness of social structure and organization, and lack of stability in the community. A concomitant by-product has been contempt for all work that does not lead to aggrandizement of the individual's personality. Material values are merely a means in the service of higher goals. To base the grandeur of the individual on material wealth is demeaning and leads to his degeneration. In short, the Spaniard's repugnance toward the Puritan's work ethic is derived from his reluctance to submit to, and be dominated by, a foreign object. Utilitarian activity sullies his dignity. On the other hand, worthy leisure is ennobling. He finds solidarity with other human beings, not in work, but in the undertaking of a "mission." For this reason, he set out to conquer new lands in America, to realize new missions, missions which would fail because the value system imposed by Western Europe did not coincide with his view of life (p. 229).

In this connection, Zea cannot resist contrasting the two Reformations. The Spanish Counter Reformation, he maintains, strove to enhance Christianity and to incorporate all the emergent nations within its orbit. The Protestant Reformation was more interested in stressing the role of the individual in its most absolute sense. If the Spanish concept had triumphed, Europe would not have been fragmented into so many religious sects and nationalities (p. 239). The Western Reformation was more interested in fomenting a critical, individualistic spirit than in extending and strengthening the Christian community. Yet an inconsistency seems to emerge: Zea states that the Spaniard came to the New World in search of gold, as well as for the greater glory of God. He quotes Marcel Bataillon: ". . . in the Indies [the Iberian] seeks precious spices, but also the glory of God" (p. 241). When one notes the sequence in which these two goals are presented (1—gold, 2—God), one has reason to question the validity of the entire structure which has been erected so painstakingly by apologists for Spain, namely, the thesis which places emphasis on "glory," "fame," "mission," etc.

Nevertheless, one point bears stressing. The Iberian penetration into the New World was characterized by political, economic, and cultural aims. The Anglo-Saxon expansion, by contrast, was primarily economic and political, and only secondarily cultural. The "greater glory of God" had another meaning in the case of the Spaniard: domination of land and wealth. Whereas in the North American colonies the Indians were decimated, in Spanish America they were "incorporated." Again, in the latter case, one must not lose sight of the fact that the motivation was not purely religious. The natives constituted an abundant source of labour supply so that the Spanish settlers could continue to persist in their attitude of disdain for manual labour. On the other side of the coin, the role of the early missionaries cannot be underestimated. Perhaps it is they who can be considered as the true representatives of the "other" Spain, the Spain of the Erasmists, who incorporated new peoples into the Christian World.

One may well speculate at this point as to the relative importance of the native component of the Latin American personality configuration. Did the characteristics generally associated with the Indians, especially as these manifest themselves in the mestizo, contribute to the "marginality" of Spanish America? At least one noted historian has considered the indigenous spirit to be the antithesis of the vital optimism characteristic of the Renaissance. The Indians "conceived history to be fatality and catastrophe. Nothing was more alien to Indian mentality than the western idea of progress."[50] Although Zea does not consider this aspect in the formulation of his thesis, preferring to couch the problem in terms of the conflict between Iberian Catholicism and mercantile expansionist Protestantism, the indigenous factor and its possible influence—no matter how minimal—cannot be discounted.

* * * * *

Ironically enough, claims Zea, the tables have been turned. The same spirit which originally characterized Europe's domination of non-Western peoples, has in more recent times been monopolized by the United States. The latter now dominates Europe; the continent which formerly exploited marginal peoples now experiences a feeling of "marginality." The psychological compensatory mechanism, always at work, has resulted in assertions of European cultural superiority.

[50] Mariano Picón-Salas, *De la conquista a la independencia* (Mexico: Fondo de Cultura Económica, 1944), p. 24.

Zea quotes a number of spokesmen (e.g., Guido Piovone, Paul Rivet, and Antony Babel) who maintain that Europe represents the classical and Christian tradition, as opposed to the bourgeois, capitalist spirit characteristic of the United States; a Christian community poised to resist the advances of both aggressive American capitalism and the non-Christian culture of the Soviets.[51] Zea sees this Christian humanism as best personified by the Iberian spirit. This seems to be the main thrust of the argument at this point. One has the feeling that Europe is getting its just reward for not having followed in the footsteps of Christian humanism, Spanish variety. Zea's romantic idealization of the Iberian spirit can hardly be justified in view of such outstanding examples of this spirit as the Franco regime in Spain, Portugal's record under Salazar's dictatorship, and Brazil's treatment of political dissidents, just to mention a few. Yet, in all justice to Zea, it must be said that he does condemn imperialistic policy, regardless of the source. "Many Europeans who condemn United States imperialism do not hesitate, in turn, to justify French or English imperialism, or that of any country" (p. 171). However, Zea's postulate remains vulnerable. He quotes with approval from M. F. Sciacca's *La filosofía hoy*, which contains a chapter on Latin American philosophy: "Thanks to the Hispanic, Christian, Catholic origin, Latin America seems called upon to continue authentic European culture, which is beyond the reach of the United States" (p. 172).

Yet, in an earlier work Zea had hinted at the negative influence exerted by the Iberian spirit, a spirit which had tried to "Christianize modernity" and failed, instead of "modernizing Christianity." Spain and Portugal had opted for the past, and dragged the New World along with them—in opposition to the "modern spirit" which sought to utilize Christianity in the service of building a future for the individual, both materially and politically.[52] Spain forced man to choose between salvation in this world and that of the next, between Christianity and the Modern Age, thus disrupting his totality. But man's individual freedom was not necessarily in conflict with Iberian Christianity; nor did his welfare here on earth have to be incompatible with salvation in the next world. This was an unnecessary dichotomy, but reconciling these two viewpoints was apparently impossible of achievement in Latin America (p. 162).

The Spanish Erasmists—to further illustrate the point—were opposed to making "modern" individualism an end in itself; they conceived the individualistic spirit to be a means in the service of the Christian community. But Spain, obsessed by its dream of unifying Europe under Catholicism and placing the interests of Christianity

---

[51] *América en la historia*, pp. 161-62.
[52] *Latinoamerica y el mundo* (Caracas: Universidad Central de Venezuela, 1960), pp. 158-59.

above the diversity of particular interests, found even its own Erasmists too hard to swallow. Spain refused to become "commercialized." Resting on the laurels of its impoverished nobility, it did nothing to encourage the growth of a middle class. Ironically, the Catholic Church— whether it wanted to or not—was helping Calvin by blocking attempts at a liberalization of Spain, a fact attested to by the absence of an active bourgeoisie. Spain was therefore considered "unfit" to be a worthy competitor; its "marginality" was established and transferred to the New World.[53]

Spanish America has borne the same relationship to the United States that Spain has had with western Europe. In both instances the "marginal" areas were viewed as being opposed to "progress." Yet there is an important difference: Spanish America, possibly because it had come upon the world arena at a much later date and had more catching up to do, attempted modernization much more quickly, relatively speaking, than did the mother country. In fact the history of the Spanish American countries can be said to be a record of attempts at Westernization, i.e., adopting the Western spirit and technology. Emancipation of the Spanish colonies had emulated Western models. The civil wars of the first half of the nineteenth century were fought between those who wanted "progress" à la Europe and the United States, and those who wished to abide by the old order, inherited from Spain.

Dictatorships came into being in the name of instituting "order" for the sake of eventual "progress." These same dictatorships received the support of the United States which saw in them a helpful ally in the pursuit of its own economic interests. However, there was always one overriding consideration that had to be kept in mind: the United States preferred to relegate Latin America to the role of a source of supply of raw materials.

This posed an obvious dilemma, a clash between two products of "Western" culture, i.e., liberal democracy on the one hand, and technological and economic expansion on the other. The resistance of the United States (and of the Western World in general) to the process of Latin American "Westernization" resulted in a crisis of Western values. Sovereignty and the right to self-determination of peoples were derived from the liberal ideals of the West. And now the West had to choose: either to abandon its ideals for the sake of protecting its economic interests, or give up its economic domination in order to continue being the leader in deeds, not only in words, in an attempt to further these democratic ideals. A difficult choice indeed! (pp. 189-91).

This contradiction has also been perceived with increasing frequency by the "marginal" non-West. Latin America and the Third World, generally, note with growing awareness that they do not have to

---

[53] *América en la historia*, p. 261.

imitate the West any longer in every respect. Latin America, in particular, must become aware of other positive, non-Western values for possible utilization. In this way, argues Zea, Latin America can become a bridge between the conquerors and the conquered, and effect a sort of cultural *mestizaje* or hybridization. This is essentially the content of Zea's dream, the message he would transmit to the world, and the role he would assign to his continent. Latin America would perhaps discover its own essence in the process—partaking of Western culture, but without forsaking non-Western history. It would no longer try to be what it is not, with the resultant feelings of frustration and inferiority. Perhaps in this way it might even be able to reconcile Christianity with modernity (p. 192).

The new nationalism, characteristic of the Third World (e.g., India, Indonesia, Africa) for the past several decades, was unfurled long ago in Latin America, claims Zea. Hence Latin America has much to offer.[54] The problems faced by the new nations have been known to Latin Americans for more than a century.[55] Our past experiences, our yearnings and frustrations, have served to make us realize that we are similar to the peoples of the Third World. We each have our possibilities as well as our circumstantial limitations.

We cannot be content any longer in our present role of supplying raw materials. We must be masters of our own wealth. In order to achieve this, the basic problem to be solved is the question of land reform (p. 67). The land must be made productive, land which has for so long been in the hands of feudal landowners or foreign companies.

Latin Americans have to wage their struggle on a dual front: against their own feudal class, as well as against the economic expansionism of the United States. The United States will always loom as a threat because it will claim that any possible intervention in Latin American countries is necessary in order to resist the inroads of Communism. But whether the co-called Cold War between the United States and the Soviet Union "heats up" or cools off to "detente" proportions, the big fish will always devour the little fish. "How long," exclaims Zea, "will we continue to be little fish?" (p. 90).

D. Latin America, the United States, and the Third World

In one of his latest works,[56] Zea attempts to weave together all the threads to be found in his earlier writings, and to amplify further a number of themes previously touched upon in his history of ideas and

---

[54] (Ironically, Africa seems to have become "Latinamericanized," but not in the sense advocated by Zea. One need only take note of the plethora of military dictatorships on the Black Continent.)

[55] *Latinoamérica y el mundo*, p. 52.

[56] *Dialéctica de la conciencia americana* (Mexico: Alianza Editorial Mexicana, 1976).

their philosophical interpretation. Zea is essentially concerned with the search for meaning that can be gleaned from a critical analysis of Latin American history. As he has suggested, Latin American philosophy will save Western culture, which finds itself presently in a spiritual crisis. The great hope, entertained by Zea, is that Latin American philosophy will arrest the process of dehumanization suffered by contemporary man. An American critic has complained that Zea, in writing history, should stick to the facts without attempting to interpret them.[57] Zea counters by insisting that he is indeed interested in "ideology," "meta-history," or "metaphilosophy," as charged. Raat's insistence on being "empirical," or refraining from meditating on the implications of historical facts, is itself, according to Zea, an expression of an ideology, a way of looking at the world—in this case, a technological world viewed technologically. This is the world of the Cold War, of professional violence, of which "technical," calculating and mechanical professionals are simply by-products.[58]

Zea is still searching for instrumentalities in this work—hopefully to be found as a result of historical and philosophical awareness—whereby the Mexican, and the Latin American generally, will be able to embark upon a more rational course of action, and no longer act in a subordinate role under the domination of foreign interests.

As in earlier works, Zea refers to Hegel, apparently his favourite and most oft-quoted philosopher. Hegel had spoken of the future of the Spirit and its efforts to achieve its fullest development as awareness and realization of freedom. However, as is well known, Hegel had considered America to be outside the march of history, at least insofar as history was equivalent to awareness. For history must be an awareness of goals to be achieved if it is to attain a degree of authenticity. Freedom is the ultimate end of history; the efforts of the Spirit to manifest and fulfil itself freely gave rise to history in the first place. The Spirit, in its journey toward a greater measure of freedom, passes through various stages. At first, a dim awareness of this freedom was characteristic of Oriental peoples. Only the despot was free and dominant in this case; the great masses of people were still subservient and slavish. In the next stage, that of the Greeks, there was a slightly greater degree of freedom—for the entire Greek people, but not for non-Greeks. Under Christianity, the awareness of freedom reached its zenith. But this was only an awareness which was not fully realized until the triumph of the French Revolution. Europe personified this Spirit at the moment, maintained Hegel. However, the Spirit would continue to

---

[57] William D. Raat, "Ideas e historia en México: un ensayo sobre metodología," in *Latino América, Anuario, Estudios, Latinoamericanos, No. 3* (Mexico: Universidad Nacional Autónoma de México, 1970). A similar criticism is suggested by the same author in an earlier article (see footnote 16 of this chapter).

[58] *Conciencia americana*, p. 11.

seek ever new opportunities for further development of the conscious awareness of the freedom principle.

It is at this point that America enters the picture. America was the continent of the future, maintained Hegel, where this increased awareness would take place. The German philosopher proved correct in his prophecy. A century later, the drive toward greater freedom materialized: the concept was carried to the most remote corners of the globe. Newly discovered peoples began to clamour for the various freedoms which the Western World had hitherto claimed for its own exclusive use.

The conflict involved in the struggle for such recognition, maintains Zea, has its origin in America. Once again we come upon a familiar theme: the United States, fighting to secure and hold fast to its freedoms—wrested from the Old World—now refuses to recognize the right to these freedoms which other "less developed" countries would also like to claim as their own.

Zea is here attempting to write a philosophy of history, specifically Latin American history, as a concrete expression of the history of humanity in its effort to achieve the goal of freedom. This philosophy of history is mirrored in the conflict between the two Americas: North and South. On the one hand, the United States proclaims freedom, but denies it to others. On the other, Latin America strives valiantly to achieve it. The result for the United States is a realization on its part of the contradiction in which it finds itself enmeshed: the discrepancy between its ideals and its interests. Zea is convinced that the example set by Latin America in its attempts to attain its goals will be observed with considerable interest by other countries the world over which are only now beginning to undergo experiences similar to those known to Latin America a century ago. Zea hearkens back to an old theme, namely, similarities and differences between individuals, groups, and nations. This time he seeks to improve upon it by further refining and crystallizing it, and bringing it into sharper focus in conformity with the most recent world events. Adopting sociological terminology, he speaks of the "out-group" as being a dissimilar entity which constitutes a threat to the familiar surroundings or frame of reference in the "in-group." The in-group seeks to exploit the out-group for its own purposes; the out-group, in turn, resists, and attempts to take advantage of its adversary in order to advance *its* interests. The result is conflict and reluctance or refusal to admit that the opponent is possessed of human qualities, while at the same time asserting one's own humanity (p. 30). The in-group will even go so far as to regard itself as the maximum expression of human values, the representative par excellence of "culture" and "civilization," and the model to be emulated by others. Furthermore, in order to enforce this "emulation," the "model" seeks to impose its way of life in an attempt to "civilize" and bring "culture" to "backward" countries. The reaction on the part of these "under-developed" peoples is an increased awareness of their own humanity and of others who find themselves in a similar situation.

Zea's contention—repeated in earlier works—is that the West has projected its cultural forms on a world scale and has demonstrated at the same time an infuriating blindness toward the values of other peoples, an attitude which may well be covered by the umbrella term "imperialism." To qualify for membership in the Western "club," all other nations, considered "subcultures" by the West, must meet certain requirements. Zea complains indignantly: The French, the English, or the Germans, for example, never had to justify *their* condition as human beings; they supposedly represented the "essence" of man. On the other hand, the Latin American, the African, the Asian were considered "accidental" expressions of mankind, and therefore had to render an account of their existence and justify their claim to humanity (p. 34).

The post-World War II era changed all this. Colonial peoples are no longer a "project" to be realized for the benefit of the "more advanced" nations in the name of an abstract, mythical goal called "divinity," "destiny," "spirit," or "civilization" (pp. 40-41). The more sensitive elements of the Western World have since realized that colonial peoples have a will of their own, and that they can no longer be used to promote the "progress" of Europe and the United States. Zea prefers to think that this growing historical awareness points the way to a modification in the total structure of world organization. Philosophically, it represents a transition from the concrete to the universal, a realization on the part of individual segments of the world community of the need to recognize the existence of the whole (pp. 45-46). On a lower level of operation, i.e., in the economic sphere, the stance adopted by the Arab states with respect to their oil policy is perhaps a striking example of the realization by members of the Third World of their ability to cause a crisis to develop in Europe and North America. The tail is indeed wagging the dog!

In the course of this on-going process, Latin America cannot fail to remain unaffected. It has always struggled to realize those values so proudly proclaimed by Europe and the United States, but paradoxically, instead of helping Latin America in its quest, these have been determined to maintain the status quo. In fact, the United States, especially, has always sought its allies from within the Latin American conservative groups that were similarly interested in preventing change. It was the liberal element which had always wanted to join the mainstream and become "modernized" that was viewed by the United States as an obstacle in the way of its own expansionist policies.

At the turn of the century, Zea goes on to explain, new middle-class groups emerged to replace the old bourgeoisie which had served merely as an instrument to be utilized by international capitalistic interests. These new groups were aware of the need to do battle on two fronts: against their "own" oligarchies and against the forces of Western imperialism. As a consequence, they would have to initiate a new policy, characterized by a "defensive nationalism," i.e., resisting exploitation by foreign interests. At the same time they would realize the need for agrarian reform which would put an end to this exploitation, raise the standard of living, and create, thereby, the possibilities for developing a consumer market on the domestic front.

To sum up: the nature of Mexican and, by extension, Latin American identity, is intimately tied in with the solution to two types of conflict which Zea designates as: (1) vertical, in the sense of Marxist class struggle within a given country, and (2) horizontal, i.e., the struggle between colonial peoples and the more developed, imperialist nations. In a very real sense, these two categories are closely related. For example, Latin America provides an excellent illustration of a situation wherein "native" conservative elements joined the forces of the expansionist Western nations.[59] In doing so, they placed themselves in direct opposition to the progressive sectors of their society which aspired to attain the benefits of "Westernization," a process which would have given rise to new competitive pressures and which, therefore, ran counter to the interests of the West. In the Western view, Latin America was to provide opportunities for the expansion of *others*.

The rise of a Latin American middle class, the result of Westernization, carried with it a realization of the need for industrialization. Since this implied a departure from the exploitation of land, it posed a threat to the old landed oligarchies. As a result, the middle class found itself in a conflict situation vis-à-vis the oligarchy, as well as foreign economic interests. Moreover, Latin American industrialization found itself in a dilemma. Industrialization requires markets for consumption of products. Where were these to be found? All of the world markets had already been pre-empted. As to the home market, who would purchase the newly-manufactured products, in view of the low standard of living? There was simply no buying power with which to effect transactions. This was the genesis of Latin American economic nationalism, a phenomenon which was to spread to the other "have-not" nations the world over, and was to characterize the history of the twentieth century. In short, Latin America had come of age in attempting to change its status, from a position of subordination to that of an equal.

It is this particular circumstance which the philosopher must deal with in his analysis of Latin American essence, and in his attempt to solve the problems arising out of this set of conditions.[60]

---

[59] See pp. 81-82.
[60] Zea, *América como conciencia*, p. 163.

These solutions are not eternal. However, they do have a great deal in common with other solutions which the rest of mankind can possibly utilize. It is this quality which gives them a universal stamp; it is this process which makes for a greater degree of maturity and acts as an antidote to any feelings of inferiority.

In this connection, too, Zea has some harsh words for the Latin American intellectual. The latter seems to have lost sight of the fact that the formulation of theory is dictated by the need to solve particular problems. In spite of their pretensions at being abstract and universal, ideas constitute a foundation for practice in specific instances. Practice is abstracted and converted into a symbol. Theory attempts to capture and encompass by means of a reduced number of symbols the totality of multiple human experiences. Today's intellectual, maintains Zea, has made theory a sort of parlour game, and has, therefore, lost the respect and confidence of his compatriots. It is the duty of the intellectual to transform human experiences into a dependable instrument, to be used as a guide for more effective action. But instead, the intellectual has defaulted. The result has been anarchy. The man in the street is incapable of abstracting by himself the viable forms of social and moral practice. As a result, limited and selfish interests have arrogated to themselves important priorities, to the detriment of the common good (p. 173).

One wonders whether Zea is not according too much weight to the role of the intellectual in modern society. How effective can he be, for example, in a country controlled by a police state? And even though he may represent the conscience and articulate the unspoken aspirations of his fellow-man, can he be the determining factor, even at the risk of great sacrifice, which might motivate in catalytic fashion the process of much-needed change? How many intellectuals are ready and willing to become martyrs, if need be? The question is a painful one, at best. Nevertheless, Zea's idealism cannot but be admired. Man, he concludes, needs new theoretical formulations in order to give meaning to his existence. Otherwise he will be mutilated, a dehumanized automaton (p. 179).

* * * * *

This, then, is the sum and substance of the "American Tragedy" of Americans of both continents: specifically, in the case of the United States, of Americans who realize that the fruits of their own revolution have infected other peoples of the globe; the latter have been by-passed by its consequences and implications.[61] The critical question which must be answered by the United States is whether it is willing to transform its revolution into one of world-wide perspectives. Zea

[61] *Conciencia americana*, p. 85.

concludes rather pessimistically that the answer is negative. The United States, for the present, is opposed to revolutions; this would jeopardize investments and profits.

Again resorting to Hegel's dictum, Zea holds that individuals as well as nations are utilized as instruments by the Spirit which unfolds in the course of historical development. In this way, the nation reaches its maximum point of evolution, coinciding with the goals of the Spirit. But once this path is traversed and the mission "completed," so to speak, the roads diverge, the nation is left behind, and the Spirit continues on its way, manifesting itself via other nations and peoples. This is what happened, for example, in Athens, cradle of democracy, and in Rome, birthplace of the law. This is also the fate suffered by the United States. Originally a model to be followed by other nations, it has, as a result of its phenomenal growth, been transformed into a tool to be used by a minority for antirevolutionary ends.

Yet Zea does not believe that all is lost. He hopefully points to signs which indicate that there are elements within the United States which are aware of the tragic policy being pursued by that country. These are the elements which realize that the Spirit which now inspires revolutionary activity in Asia, Africa, and Latin America is the same as that which caused the American colonies to challenge British domination (p. 92). Unfortunately, these elements are still not sufficiently strong. Their voices are drowned out and overwhelmed by the more ruthless forces which, paradoxically, justify invasions (such as in the case of the Dominican Republic), supposedly in the name of helping the invaded countries achieve democratic ideals. In other words, follow the "democratic" line or suffer the consequences (p. 98).

The foreign policy of the United States was bound to evoke a reaction. The new Latin American "defensive nationalism," referred to above, was the response which would permit the participation of all social sectors in the all-embracing task of building the economy. Latin America had arrived on the historical scene too late to share in the world's booty. In fact, it had itself been part of that booty. The new nationalism set out to alter this relationship. The first step in the process was to rid the continent of the deeply entrenched oligarchies which had been responsible for taking the continent down this path of economic dependency.

Turning his attention to the Mexican scene for purposes of illustration, Zea points to the Revolution of 1910 as an outstanding example of this new relationship of forces. The Revolution was not only political but social in nature, and as such, represented a threat to North American interests. Fortunately, world conditions came to its rescue. The United States, involved in World War I, was faced by a dilemma: How could it fight to "make the world safe for democracy," how could it proclaim freedom and human dignity in Europe while, at the same time, intervening in the affairs of a country, south of its own border, a country which was, likewise, proclaiming and struggling to convert into reality the very same slogans preached in the North? This dilemma for the United States saved the Mexican Revolution (p. 156). The "Colossus of the North" could not—at least at this historical juncture—justify violent intervention.

Latin America learned another lesson, thanks to the economic crisis suffered by the United States in 1929. It realized that it would have to look for ways and means of developing self-sufficiency, and not depend on foreign interests. Mexico, Brazil, and Argentina took the lead in this respect. As was to be expected, the United States did not take kindly to these nationalist movements which were threatening to weaken its position vis-à-vis the rest of the continent. But again historical circumstances intervened to modify overt hostility on the part of the United States. World War II posed a question similar to the dilemma occasioned by its predecessor. How could a nation send in marines to keep "order" in any of the Latin American countries, if these marines resembled Nazi troops? And so one Roosevelt replaced another. The policy of the "Big Stick" had to be shelved, at least temporarily. Latin America had to be wooed, its support mobilized in the war against the Axis powers (p. 179).

It was precisely this situation which enabled Lázaro Cárdenas—as an exponent of nascent "defensive nationalism"—to nationalize the oil industry, while the United States stood by helplessly without daring to retaliate with repressive measures. The United States ambassador, Josephus Daniels, was obliged to admit that Cárdenas' actions were simply a Mexican version of the New Deal (p. 185). In short, this was merely an attempt to develop an independent national bourgeoisie with its own prospects for development, one which would be more than just an appendage to a foreign economy. Cárdenas wished to make Mexico a partner in the corporation, even if only a junior partner!

Unfortunately, the policies of Cárdenas did not succeed. The Mexican bourgeoisie put its class interests above the national weal. Although the governing class claimed to act in the name of the masses, it did not permit their creative participation in the economic development of the nation—a fact perceived by Zea more than two decades ago, when he wrote that the new Mexican bourgeoisie was increasing production at the expense of the lower classes "in order to maintain its independence vis-à-vis the interests of the Western bourgeoisie."[62] Zea's fears and suspicions have since been confirmed—suspicions shared by many of his contemporaries.[63] The new bourgeoisie, having pushed the old landowning interests aside, has lapsed into the role of collaborator with the expansionist interests of the United States. It has

[62] *Conciencia de México*, p. 74.
[63] For example, Carlos Fuentes, the noted novelist.

betrayed the ideals of the Revolution by attempting to curb the increased demands of the working classes, both rural and urban. It has lost its original anti-imperialist orientation.

Nationalist aspirations received a new boost at the end of World War II. Colonial peoples of Asia and Africa who had witnessed the defeats and humiliations suffered by the white man at the hands of totalitarian regimes realized that he was vulnerable. He was no longer Man par excellence, a fact perceived by Latin America as well. Yet the situation was now made more complicated by a new element which had been injected into the picture. A new power had emerged to challenge the United States. The Cold War could now be utilized by the nation to the north to justify intervention in Latin America in the name of combatting Communism.[64]

The appearance of economic nationalism in what were formerly colonial countries as a "response" to the "challenge" of foreign interests resulted in a choice between two alternatives: either the new nationalists accepted the role assigned to them by the new empire, or else they would be accused of being Communists—a choice faced also by Latin Americans.

However, Zea appears to oversimplify the issue. It is surely possible to be a nationalist in what was at one time an exploited area, and to attempt to work for the welfare of that area even though such efforts might coincide with anti-imperialist policy, without necessarily being in the Communist camp. The nationalist has frequently been faced by this dilemma, precisely because there are Communists to be found in anticolonial movements. He may be a representative of the middle class, and is content to cooperate with left-wing, lower-class elements in a common struggle against foreign economic domination. Yet once this struggle appears to be making headway, the nationalists and the Communists come to a parting of the ways. Recent history affords not a few examples of conflict between the two: each wants to capture control of the situation and one or the other is ousted as a result. Communist versus Nationalist China, and the Middle East (e.g., Egypt, Syria, Iraq), illustrate the tug-of-war between these two forces. As far as Latin America is concerned, only in Cuba did the Communist Left triumph, and the leftist-inclined "nationalist" bourgeois elements were pushed out of the picture.

The point to be remembered—and Zea goes to great lengths to explain the Cuban episode—is that "the Cuban Revolution aspired to the same human goals as the Guatemalan Revolution of 1944, the Mexican Revolution of 1910, and the American Revolution of 1776" (p. 274). But the heirs of 1776 did everything possible to brake the efforts of the twentieth-century revolutionaries.

[64] *Conciencia americana*, p. 248.

The implication is clear: the United States, by its anti-Castro policy, forced Fidel to assume a more leftist position than had, perhaps, been contemplated at the outset by the leaders of the anti-Batista rebellion—a point not original with Zea. However, this may be more than mere speculation. After all, Zea reminds us, Castro could point to the Mexican and Guatemalan episodes. Cuba was not going to duplicate *that* experience.

The United States had to respond to the Castro phenomenon. The Alliance for Progress was the answer to the Cuban challenge. Latin America was no longer a colonial area, ripe for exploitation. It was now invited "to be an active part of the new and powerful empire" (p. 283). The Alliance was an insurance policy, and the United States was prepared to pay premiums in order to prevent Latin America from embarking upon other, more dangerous paths.

But this was precisely the difficulty, notes Zea. All the lofty sounding, well-intentioned projects envisaged by the Alliance for Progress were to be carried out by dependable businessmen, landowners, and investors. Social legislation, land reform, improvements in programs of health, education, and general welfare—all would be effected within the basic economic structure. Those in charge of the Alliance could hardly be expected to allow meaningful changes to be made within that structure—changes which might conceivably alter class relationships. Indeed, President Kennedy, quixotic perhaps in this untenable position, incurred the ire of his own right-wing critics.[65]

The conflict between the anti-imperialist nationalist and the Communist, referred to above, seemed to have been resolved in the Cuban situation. According to Zea, one phase developed into the other, at least insofar as Castro and his followers were concerned. They were "liberals, nationalists, bourgeois, but in their struggle against imperialism, they had discovered wider goals, more in keeping with a new society, foreseen by Marx and Lenin."[66] In other words, it would be too mechanical to conceive of the bourgeoisie as an undifferentiated, homogeneous whole. Instead, one should think in terms of segments within this class: some going one way, i.e., exerting every effort to preserve their interests within the framework of reform; others becoming more radicalized and advancing the conflict situation to more critical stages.[67]

[65] The Left in Latin America could not fail to oppose the Alliance. Utilizing a play on words, they talked about an Alliance which *stops* progress (Alianza *para* el progreso). Unfortunately, *para* is both a preposition and a verb—probably an oversight on the part of someone in Washington who did not know his Spanish too well.

[66] *Conciencia americana*, p. 293. For a detailed account of the curious evolution from "petit bourgeois adventurism" to Marxist socialism, as related by Castro himself, see Maurice Halperin, *The Rise and Decline of Fidel Castro* (Berkeley: University of California Press, 1972). See especially the reactions forthcoming from Moscow and Peking, respectively.

[67] The case of the centrist Christian Democrats of Chile before and after the tragic end of the Allende government would seem to be illustrative of this tendency.

Zea considers the Cuban Revolution as just one more instance in a series of similar upheavals throughout the world, especially in Asia and Africa (e.g., Algeria), in which the peoples of the Third World have finally matured sufficiently to attempt to break the hold of Western imperialism. The Cuban case merely serves to illustrate the fact that those Latin American regimes which try to follow the line of bourgeois nationalist liberalism eventually clash with United States foreign policy. Even the Alliance for Progress was viewed by the dominant financial interests in the States as "an instrument in the service of communism."[68] Latin American oligarchies were themselves opposed to the land reform proposed in the charter of the Alliance.

The result was a decided step backward. Every attempt at liberal reform, no matter how timid, was bound to evoke the charge of pro-Communism by the United States. Juan Bosch in Santo Domingo, João Goulart in Brazil, Fernando Belaúnde in Peru—all fell victim to this obsession. The main point to remember, and emphasized repeatedly by Zea, is that the intransigence of the United States makes possible, if not inevitable, further inroads in the direction of Communist successes (p. 309). Zea is sad, rather than angry. The United States which had always unfurled the banner of freedom and dignity in its confrontation with totalitarianism now behaves in a manner which strongly resembles this self-same totalitarianism (p. 311).[69]

*   *   *   *   *

Zea is not a professional U.S.-baiter. More than two decades ago he asked whether the United States would be able to create new institutions which would bring into harmony its own interests and those of other peoples, in accordance with the ideals of freedom and democracy—principles which it had itself proclaimed, but utilized subsequently to justify its expansionist policies. Those who criticize the United States, he wrote, do not attack the ideals and principles, but the economic interests for which the principles act as a smokescreen. Stated succinctly, there seems to be an inverse ratio between the success of material expansion and the decline of moral pretensions.[70] Are the American people aware of this dilemma? asks Zea. If they are, they should face up to it and effect a readjustment by creating new institutions with which to resolve the conflict. "This is the hope that we have, those of us who have admired and still admire the United States, its people who created liberal and democratic institutions" (p. 75).

Zea has felt all along that the Latin American must project an image of the ideal which he should strive to attain. He considers that

[68] *Conciencia americana*, p. 299.
[69] The Carter administration has attempted to erase this unfavourable image. The Panama Canal negotiations and the withholding of military aid from dictatorial *juntas* are but two examples of this development.
[70] *America en la conciencia de Europa* (Mexico: Los Presentes, 1955), pp. 72-73.

the United States has achieved in the realm of the concrete, whereas the Latin American moves about in the world of the abstract, and continues to wait without resolving his problems. If man conceives history to be a continuous process, involving the past, present, and future, the Latin American, by contrast, looks upon the present as lacking a beginning and devoid of future goals. The Latin American has, up to this point in time, rejected his past, and has been unable to plan for the future.[71] His task is to confront and control the future, and not resign himself passively to whatever may develop. One has the feeling that Zea is quite exasperated as he pleads that Latin Americans should not depend on their past. "The past," he exclaims, "is what should depend on our present."[72]

Well might one ask at this point, in comparing the two continents, whether the differences in attitudes to be found in Latin America and the United States, respectively, are merely the result of cultural traditions and the force of ideas, or rather, the consequence of what may be alluded to as the "culture of poverty" in one case, and the development of capitalism in the other. In other words, is it only the so-called Spanish heritage (i.e., the Iberian Catholic tradition) which has moulded the Latin American "life style," i.e., the entire complex of socioeconomic conditions? Speaking in a speculative vein, would Latin American "humanism" and human conviviality undergo modification or even survive, if a change in economic relations were to take place, i.e., if Latin America were to develop in a manner similar to that of the United States? To Zea's credit, be it said that he has not forgotten that economic interests lurk behind apparently "abstract" ideas, and that the ideologies of social groups in power are related to their property and privilege.

Zea has proclaimed repeatedly that the United States has been the source of Latin American inferiority. Each continent has suffered from partial visions and incomplete perspectives. The interest of the United States in Latin America has always been materialistic, complains Zea. (Has any country ever acted otherwise, vis-à-vis its neighbours?) Latin America, making use of its compensatory mechanisms, has struck back, considering itself the maximum expression of spiritual culture. Each half of the hemisphere has denied the culture of the other. Each half has brought the humanity of the other into question. Each America has emphasized that part of its personality which *seemed* most characteristic, because such emphasis was in accordance with its program.[73]

Perhaps both Americas possess similar qualities, but their projects gave rise to the differences between them. The result, accentuated today, has been that each apparently possesses qualities which the other

---

[71] *Latinoamérica y el mundo*, p. 138.
[72] *La filosofía como compromiso* (Mexico: Tezontle, 1952), p. 214.
[73] *América como conciencia*, p. 145.

lacks—a common assertion. The Uruguayan essayist, Alberto Zum Felde, has suggested in this connection an injection of the quality found wanting in one, yet abundant in the other, namely, a few drops of poetry for the North American, and a few drops of optimism and practical "know-how" for the Latin American—but only a few drops![74]

If it is agreed that philosophy is a rationale which is utilized in order to justify a way of life, then it becomes easier to be tolerant of the differences which separate the two Americas. The United States, from the very beginning, adopted a pragmatic attitude, since the domination of the natural environment was of immediate interest. By contrast, in Latin America ethical and political conduct demanded prompt attention. In each case European philosophy was adapted to the needs of the moment. It can be said that the United States acted in accord with a present already formed and which had to be preserved, whereas Latin America acted with a view to the future, still to be realized. The result, as has been seen, embraced the predominance of scientific and technical values, on the one hand, and esthetic and religious values, on the other.

American philosophy, both north and south, is still characterized by problems, the solutions to which have not yet crystallized. It is, therefore, still in the process of development and on the road to maturity. Is this a sign of inferiority? asks Zea. Not at all, since this maturity, waiting to be realized, is an indication of possibility which mature cultures no longer possess.[75]

With the world picture as a background, Zea finally asks: What is the future of Latin American nationalism? Is it condemned to failure? It would appear that this nationalism, largely economic in nature— especially in the twentieth century—is traversing a path similar to that of the nineteenth. For in both instances the Latin American bourgeoisie cannot do anything which the powerful neighbour to the north does not want it to do. It must content itself with existing in the shadow of the financial master. If yesterday the middle classes of Latin America assisted foreign interests by exporting raw materials to be exploited, today they will help by converting their small industrial establishments into subsidiaries of international capitalism. Instead of pressing for the industrialization of the continent for the welfare of *all* Latin Americans, as was the initial hope, they appear to be satisfied to assume a subordinate position in the grand design for the benefit of

[74] Alberto Zum Felde, *El problema de la cultura americana* (Buenos Aires: Editorial Losada, 1943), pp. 115-16. This myth has also been exploded in recent decades. Latin American businessmen are not at all "inferior" to those of the United States. In fact, they have displayed a remarkable facility in avoiding payment of taxes—a fact which has earned for them no end of esteem and affection (see David FitzHugh, "Whatever Happened to the New Dialogue with Latin America?" *Saturday Review*, October 18, 1975, p. 10).

[75] *La esencia de lo americano*, p. 48.

international industrialism which, of course, is controlled by the United States. The net result will continue to be economic underdevelopment for Latin America. It is therefore the task of the new, emerging social groups, such as professionals, intellectuals, peasants, and workers—aware of their marginal position—to break the chain of dependency and subservience to a United States-dominated economic system. Such action, implies Zea, will be the result of an increased awareness, one which realizes that authentic liberalism and economic nationalism will have to coincide with the policies of revolutionary socialism. "The ideals of Bolívar and Martí were the same as those of the revolutionaries of our day."[76]

The new middle class which makes its living without exploiting others, and which is itself an object of exploitation, must take stock of its position in society, and realize that it has nothing in common with the large international bourgeoisie which victimizes it. It is this same middle class which must link its destiny with that of the great mass of workers who are likewise victims of exploitation. In addition, two new allies can be counted on to share in this awakened consciousness: the militant elements of the Church as well as the revolutionary elements to be found among the military. No longer are the Church and the army to be viewed automatically as supporters of the status quo. Brazil and Peru illustrate the point. In any case, the shark can no longer coexist with the sardines.[77]

For decades the Latin American bourgeoisie attempted to imitate the experience of the North American and European bourgeoisie, namely, to achieve an equilibrium of interests, represented by various social groups. But to no avail. The very interests of Europe and the United States precluded this possibility. In the process of taking moral and intellectual inventory, Latin America has become aware of the fact that not only are the lower classes within a given country abused by those above; less developed nations are exploited by the more developed. Both forms of exploitation must be resisted. Zea, therefore, calls for an awakened consciousness on the part of all the underdeveloped nations of the earth. The peoples, not only of Latin America, but also of Asia, Africa, and Oceania, must perceive the designs of the common enemy. Latin America is thus beginning to realize that its own struggle assumes global dimensions. In facing up to the United States, it is confronting a colossus whose might has extended throughout the entire world. Zea's philosophic posture now takes on strong political and economic overtones. His humanism—the goal which has motivated all of his writing—is to be achieved through conscious, purposeful struggle. The new humanism, he believes, will

[76] *Conciencia americana*, p. 324.
[77] Juan José Arévalo, *Fábula del tiburón y las sardinas* (Buenos Aires: Editorial Palestra, 1961).

emerge as a result of the dialectical interplay between what the Western World has claimed for itself and that which it has denied to others. Man who is colonized is little more than a material object, an instrumentality to be utilized. This colonized "thing" will regain humanity in the process of liberating itself. The new humanism, if it is to be really authentic, will embrace *all* men, including Europeans and North Americans. And concluding his remarks, Zea quotes Franz Fanon, the Black revolutionary: "For Europe, for ourselves, and for humanity, comrades, we must turn over a new leaf, we must work out new concepts, and try to set afoot a new man."[78]

* * * * *

In a recent publication[79] Zea re-emphasizes to a large extent what he has written on previous occasions, with specific reference to the Third World. Once again, he insists, the history of Latin America must be viewed, not within the confines of that of the Western World, but rather in the wider, more universal context of the development of the emerging countries of the Third World. The West has utilized both areas for its own benefit; the interconnectedness between the two becomes obvious: their similarity of interests, the problems common to both, resulting from a long record of exploitation, and the possible solutions which would put an end to their dependency role.

The very terms "Latin America" and "Third World," suggests Zea, are a reminder of this dependency. These are designations invented by the West. "Latin America" is the creation of Napoleon III, having come into being on the eve of France's venture into Mexico (p. 14). As for "Third World," this appeared in Western vocabulary after World War II. Again it was France which paved the way. Postwar France, forced out of Africa, attempted to pose as the "big brother" of the former colonies, and in an effort to follow an independent policy vis-à-vis both the United States and the Soviet Union, began to use the term "Third World" with increasing frequency.

The point is, according to Zea, that both designations were invented by the Old World in order to realize imperialistic ambitions. At the present moment, however, the two areas in question have turned the tables, so to speak, and have accepted the respective terms in order to resist Western intentions and realize their own dreams (p. 16).

It would seem that Zea is attributing an inordinate degree of importance to nomenclature in this connection. The basic issue,

[78] Franz Fanon, *The Wretched of the Earth* (New York: Grove Press Inc., 1963), p. 316, quoted in Zea, *Conciencia americana*, p. 345. In this connection, the visits of Mexico's former President Luis Echeverría to the countries of the Third World, as well as his public utterances in support of their aspirations, would seem to give additional weight to Zea's thesis.

[79] *Latinoamérica: Tercer Mundo* (Mexico: Editorial Extemporáneos, 1977).

namely resistance to colonialism, is sufficiently valid, forceful, and convincing not to need further embellishment by resorting to a rather unnecessary explanation of the origin of geographic names. Far more persuasive is Zea's argument, advanced in earlier works, to the effect that the colonial peoples have appropriated the ideals (not merely the names given them) of the Western World, and have made them their own, in the face of the latter's opposition.

Latin America, claims Zea, in spite of having adopted the culture, language, and religion of its colonizers, has never been accepted by them. The Third World, too, finds itself in a similar position. The two areas have much in common. Latin America is, therefore, part of the Third World (p. 22).

The above formula is highly attractive, but seems too facile an explanation, too simple a package. There are too many variables which impede easy agreement and acceptance. Zea has not demonstrated that Spain has not "accepted" Spanish America (not Latin America), or that Portugal has not done likewise with respect to Brazil. And what does "accept" mean? In what sense? Politically? Economically? Perhaps Zea's criticism carries greater weight as far as the relationship between the United States and Latin America is concerned. But then it is no longer a question of "culture, language and religion of its colonizers."

Nor does the Third World itself present a monolithic picture. From a political point of view, for example, involving the practice of capitalist, liberal democracy of the First World, or the socialism of the Second, there is a wide array of diverse models to choose from, including undisguised dictatorships that mouth "anti-imperialist" slogans. True, the Third World, as Zea says, has appropriated the ideals of the Western World. It has also inherited many of its aberrations. There are as many rifts and contradictions in the First World as there are in the Second, as each strives to gain or maintain influence in the Third. To speak, therefore, of the Third World as though it were one undifferentiated whole is to be guilty of oversimplification.

Zea resorts to a psychological analogy as he repeats a familiar theme, one involving the identity of colonial peoples: in the case of the Third World as well as that of Latin America, the natives aspired to be like the conqueror, the master, identified as the father-figure. In the process, the heritage of the past was rejected, the mother-image or subjugated native denied. The colonial élite, especially, sought to emulate the model set by the foreign oppressor. Yet, Zea reminds us again, this élite will never share on an equal basis in the management of the colonial enterprise. Its members may be appointed as local or even national managers, but they will never really get close to the centres of international power. They will fill the role of servants, never that of partners. They will continue to strive "to be like their supposed father, while refusing to be like their authentic mother" (p. 25). Of course, some countries (e.g., Viet Nam, Cuba) have refused to be the tail to the capitalist kite and have embarked upon the socialist path.

The concept "developing country" implies an operation within the framework of international capitalism. The so-called local bourgeoisie, unlike that of the capitalist West, will have to exploit its "own" natives, rather than "other" foreign people. Development, then, will not put an end to the dependency cycle (p. 28). The Third World will thus continue to depend upon the Western bloc of nations, unless, of course, it elects the socialist road. At this point, Zea is quick to point out that the road to socialism may involve another set of "dependencies" in the making. One can only hope—and one suspects that Zea does too—that once the Gordian knot of political and economic domination is broken, situations involving "vertical dependency" will come to an end, making possible instead the growth of "horizontal solidarity" (p. 32). Unfortunately, history has thus far proved otherwise. Abuses continue to flourish even if and when the solidarity is supposedly horizontal.

Yet one should not—even though the temptation may be strong—fault Zea for his optimism. This may too easily be a cynical reaction. For Zea is a philosopher, and as such he can claim the right to be both critic and prophet. It is in this sense that he argues for an awareness of a philosophy of future possibilities, as these relate to the development of new pathways to freedom, in opposition to the perpetuation of old, or the inauguration of new, forms of domination. As long as man will continue to be viewed as a tool, utilized by other men, domination and subservience will be the order of the day. This condition, he pleads, must be replaced by human solidarity. Only then, quoting Engels, will humanity realize that great leap from the "kingdom of necessity to that of freedom" (p. 59). And freedom in this sense does not mean freedom for some at the expense of others. Freedom will no longer have to be exchanged for subsistence. For example, a worker will not have to offer his labour power to someone willing to buy it in order to continue to exist.

Quite obviously, Zea has come close to the Marxist point of view—a development noticeable in his more recent works. In this sense, he has moved away from an earlier existentialist position (but which he does not quite abandon). His affection for the Hegelian dialectic, which has never left him, is evident, especially in his on-going discussion of Latin American marginality and alienation, an alienation that derives from a condition of colonial dependence, and which can be eradicated only through liberation. The Latin American feels that he is dispossessed; he is a mere object, a thing, within the system which holds him captive. What is required now is to transform this feeling of dependency, this awareness of marginality, vis-à-vis the world upon which he depends. The colonial past is just another experience; it should be accepted and assimilated without shame or ignominy, in order to be transcended.

This Hegelian *aufhebung* will result in a more authentic humanism (p. 45).

It is in this connection, too, that Zea rejects the charge made that he is not sufficiently objective in his evaluation of the Latin American scene. It is impossible to be "objective" in this context, he argues, since the task of the Latin American philosopher is to modify historical forces and conditions which cannot be accepted. In Zea's view the philosophy of history implies that the past is not to be perceived as dead matter, as a museum filled with relics, but rather as something intimately tied in with the present. The past is not an obstacle; it is alive and vibrant, and should be assimilated into the present, so that it may be useful for the future. Knowledge of the past within a framework of colonial dependency assures its nonrepetition (pp. 64-65).

Again one must enter a caveat. It is easy to sympathize with Zea's impatience and enthusiasm. However, "microscopic objectivity," which he objects to, is not an evil in itself. It may even prevent mistakes made by enthusiastic activists. Objective research is not necessarily or exclusively the equivalent of accumulation of past techniques and experiences or the mechanical repetition of doctrine. What it can mean, instead, is the perception of possible pitfalls to be avoided, even by Zea himself, as both Latin America and the Third World break new ground in an effort to define themselves. The problem becomes especially acute in view of Zea's continual insistence that Latin America must cease imitating or operating within an older economic (i.e., Western capitalist) system, under which it has suffered endless abuse. Latin America, he states, should be the locomotive of a new system, not the caboose of an old one which is not really one's own (p. 112). And again, farther on: the Latin American is intent on discovering what is uniquely his own. "His own" is not the result of blind imitation of foreign models (p. 123).

In one of his last essays,[80] Zea considers the concept of industrial development, not only from the viewpoint of the exploited, but also from the perspective of the exploiter. The process of unending development and expansion results in a dual alienation: (1) at the colonial or "horizontal" level, where men become tools to be utilized, and (2) on the "vertical" plane, which occurs in the agent himself (i.e., the manager, master, or capitalist) who causes alienation in others.

Progress—so it has been thought—has always consisted of man's gradual ascent to the role of master of nature, removed from his slave status, i.e., his role as an instrument used by other men. Technology was to aid in this process, and was to give man an awareness of the true meaning of his existence. Unfortunately, this technology also enabled man to dominate other men who did not possess the necessary means

[80] "Sentido y contrasentido del desarrollo," in *Latinoamérica: Tercer Mundo*, pp. 125-40.

of resisting. Before long, this same progress turned out to be a double-edged sword. Always considered as an expression of continual happiness, it soon began to dominate its creator. The motor had to be kept running, otherwise the entire system would be damaged. It subsequently became necessary to *create* needs which then had to be satisfied—but never were, to the full—in order to guarantee the presence of a consumer market. Not development for man, but man for development, development per se, was now of paramount importance. The machine was running away with itself, out of control. The result? Alienation at both levels: on the poverty line, among the exploited, and among the wealthy exploiters as well.

Such is Zea's thesis: slavery on two levels (pp. 132-33). It is for this reason that the optimism of the eighteenth century has been replaced by the pessimism of the contemporary period. One crisis succeeds another. Man is dehumanized, a victim of the machine. There is a general clamour for the control and regulation of the economic development which has brought about these conditions. But Zea demurs at this point. Control only those aspects of development, he states, which apply to the wealthy, over-developed groups. Control only that which has resulted in happiness for some and misfortune for others. As for the latter (the underdeveloped and developing countries), economic development should continue, but on another basis than has hitherto been the case. This implies a process that will no longer involve domination and subordination. The message is clear: it is no longer a question of opposing the Western World and rejecting its values. Instead, it is imperative to have these values realized by those nations that have thus far failed to benefit from them (p. 134).

Development is, in short, a two-way street, an expression of the interaction of peoples. For example, the oil crisis, for better or worse, has brought to the fore a new kind of dependency relationship: not that of the colonized vis-à-vis the colonizer, the underdeveloped with respect to the developed and over-developed, but the reverse: the developed countries must now depend upon the underdeveloped p. 135). Yet this crisis, Zea believes, may eventually produce positive results. The old dominant-subordinate relationship may give way to a new horizontal relationship, based on collaboration between groups.[81] One should add at this point that it had better be so, because if not, in this particular case at least, the old relationship may well be inverted. Peoples occupying subordinate roles in the past have now learned the language of their former masters. Curiously enough, those who do not seem to be aware of this fact are some of the masters themselves. The hitherto subordinate groups are no longer content to be on the

---

[81] The fact that the developed countries now sell war materials to the underdeveloped areas of the world in exchange for oil (at the latter's insistence) can hardly be regarded as a welcome sign, i.e., a step in the direction of "horizontal solidarity."

periphery. They insist on sharing, as full partners, in the relationship involved. It behooves the super-powers and the developed countries to take note of this fact (pp. 137-38).

* * * * *

E. Existentialist Overtones

Since the Latin American experience is unique, one should begin with one's reality as a point of departure. However, being original does not mean having nothing whatsoever to do with the philosophy of others. What is called for, instead, is the judicious selection of those elements of philosophy which best suit the Latin American scene—its needs and purposes—and the subsequent arrival at solutions which are most appropriate for that scene. Therein lies the originality of the Latin American exercise. In fact, these solutions may even be equally valid for other realities, and result in an enriching experience for all concerned. We should, therefore, not be afraid of "imitation." Was Leibnitz afraid of being labelled an imitator when he followed Cartesianism?[82] Why then should Mexicans hesitate to accept the influence of others? This "imitation" takes place because urgent reality makes it imperative. It is the way in which the instrumentality is used that distinguishes "originality" from blind imitation. This was precisely why the old classical Positivism failed after it had been imported from abroad: not because the instrument wasn't any good or because the Mexicans were not knowledgeable or sufficiently professional. Failure was due to the fact that the social relationships within Mexico, as well as those in operation vis-à-vis the Western World, were left unchanged. The solution to Mexico's problems could not consist of a mere takeover in mechanical fashion of a given philosophy. It lay, rather, in the transformation—at least in part—of values and circumstances with a possible view to making these the common property of all men.

Zea repeats a familiar theme: Historicism and existentialism make possible a return to concrete Latin American reality in order to reach out eventually toward a more authoritative universality. This is a more realistic approach than the search for eternal solutions that lie outside the realm of time and space. And just as the ideas embodied in the Enlightenment constituted the justification for the political independence of the continent, the historicist approach provides the grounds for philosophic independence (p. 93). The echo of Andrés Bello's admonition continues to be heard: imitate the spirit, but not the total product of European culture.

The existentialist approach is also utilized in an attempt to discover the nature of the Latin American: his anguish and nausea, his at-

---

[82] La filosofía americana como filosofía sin más, p. 75.

tempted projects and resultant alienation, due to his subordination to others. Existentialism, like historicism, studies not the essential man, but rather man within a given situation, one in which he has to act, live and exist. In this sense, Latin Americans are beginning to understand philosophy, not as a collection of universal norms, independent of man, but as being universal precisely because it makes clear just what it is that the Latin American has in common with other men.

The strands of historicist and existentialist thought in Mexico lead back directly to what Samuel Ramos had said about Mexican culture. Mexican culture, states Zea, paraphrasing Ramos, is universal culture made "ours," or in other words, "Mexicanized." In the process, the Mexican discovers his uniqueness, and at the same time, his link in the chain of a greater humanity. In the process, too, he divests himself of his inferiority complex without replacing it by an equally undesirable superiority complex (p. 106).

The European, as a result of the world crisis, has stepped down from his pedestal from which vantage point he had always viewed himself as the archetype of everything human. Almost simultaneously, the Latin American has ripped off the mask which has covered his humanity, a mask which he had worn for decades because he fancied himself less of a man than the others. The European discovered his humanity as a result of pain and solitude. The Latin American had known this pain and solitude for centuries (p. 106). These two solitudes now appear to have met. We Latin Americans, as Octavio Paz puts it, "are for the first time in our history contemporaries of all men."[83]

Western man, now more aware of his limitations and a bit more humble, has found his encounter with the non-West (including Latin America) a painful experience. Non-Western man has hitherto been an object to be exposed, looked at, and used. Now it is the European's turn. He has never had to answer for his actions. Now *his* humanity has been brought into question and he will have to be viewed and examined. The attitude which the West has always displayed toward the non-West is paralleled in Latin America by the creole's view of the Indian, or, for that matter, the attitude of the white man toward the black in the United States. In all cases the "underdog" is considered a dehumanized "thing." But now the European has also become a thing, a robot. In the war between man and technology, the former has been devoured by the latter. Western man has become a tool in the hands of a tool, limited by the system which he has himself created, and alienated by what he has developed. This is why alienation is presently a central theme of Western philosophy. Philosophy no longer asks what man is, but how he acts or rather, how he should act in order to really be a man.

[83] *El laberinto de la soledad*, p. 150.

The implicit conclusion is that if he is to act this way, then he must take part in the creation of a more just world.

Some philosophers in the West have realized its inhumanity. The Toynbees, Sartres, and Marcuses have warned, but the world refuses to listen. In this connection Zea quotes a disciple of Sartre, Pierre Trotignon, who maintains that philosophy must assume the role of radical criticism, even of justifying change by violence, if necessary, when all else fails, since the world apparently no longer holds out hope for increasing man's humanity.[84]

One concrete manifestation of the above in the political sphere can be said to be the increased stirrings among the nations of the Third World. As Zea puts it: the system of values has been reversed. It is no longer the Western view which is being imposed upon the non-West, but that of the non-West which is imposing itself upon the conscience of Western man (p. 135). It is, in short, the humanity of others which has shown up the inadequacy of Western man's humanity. It is the resistance offered by the non-West to colonial alienation which has pointed to the self-alienation of the Westerner and to the limitations to his own freedom. In the eyes of the non-West, the European is now an object to be pushed around or aside, if he interferes with its plans and strategy to be used in writing the new history of formerly colonial peoples (p. 138).

* * * * *

A familiar complaint is heard again: We have always wanted to be like Europe, realizing Europe's dreams, repeating Western themes, even if these involve—as they do at present—desperation, alienation, nausea, etc. If it was liberal Europe yesterday, it is Communist Europe today, but it is still Europe. We are still strangers and dispossessed. We are still exiles in our own land. We must, once and for all, cut the umbilical cord, as Hector Murena has put it, in order to find our own "style."[85] We are always waiting for something to happen, for Europe to make the first move.

Only when we commit this cultural parricide, as Murena suggests, will Latin America enter the world of history. Shades of Hegel, who had also affirmed that the continent exists only in nature, but not in history. The theme is also echoed by the Venezuelan philosopher, Ernesto Mayz Vallenilla. Originality, identity, authenticity—these are all terms which betray a basic feeling of dissatisfaction and radical insecurity in the face of history.[86] The Latin American still feels that he

[84] *Filosofía sin más*, p. 133.

[85] H. A. Murena, *El pecado original de América* (Buenos Aires: Ed. Sudamericana, 1965), p. 33.

[86] Ernesto Mayz Vallenilla, "El problema de América," in *Antología de la filosofía americana contemporánea*, ed. Leopoldo Zea (Mexico: B. Costa-Amic, 1968), p. 206.

is undefined. He is the man who waits for something to happen. It is this air of permanent expectancy which characterizes the Latin American's originality—an expectancy summed up in the phrase, "not to be quite yet—permanently."[87] But this continuous air of expectancy has to be broken. The Latin American has to be prepared to face whatever may materialize. His degree of originality will emerge as a result of the way in which he utilizes his present circumstance. In the process, maintains Zea, the Latin American must cease being a tool to be exploited, a means to be utilized by the West. The New World is not something "given"; nor will it develop by chance into the Promised Land. The Latin American runs the risk of not having his New World; in fact he hasn't won it yet.

Does this imply that Latin America should follow the advice of Trotignon and destroy its oppressor? We should not destroy for the sake of destroying, replies Zea, for in doing so we are imitating Western man. The very act of destroying Western culture violently, or even our desire to destroy, shows our subordination to that culture. What we need to do, instead, is to build, and to eliminate all obstacles which stand in the way.[88] In this optimistic vein, Zea would build a world in which there will be room for Western man, but one which will avoid the dehumanizing factors that characterize *his* world.

Can philosophy be used as an instrumentality with which to discover our world and our position therein? Samuel Ramos, as has been noted earlier, was the first to attempt this approach when he formulated the thesis of a philosophy of Mexicanness. He had criticized mere imitation of European thought, but had also warned against a narrow-minded nationalism. Mexican culture, Ramos had written, was universal culture related to Mexican circumstances. Ramos had been influenced by Ortega's historicism. Zea, in turn, makes Ramos his point of departure. Yet there is an interesting difference between Zea and Ramos, one which involves the concept of "inadequacy." For Zea, Mexican inadequacy—and by extension Latin American inadequacy—is the realization of an awareness of how much has yet to be assimilated in order to achieve an authentic, universal culture. In Ramos, as Villegas points out, "inadequacy" was a negative factor; for Zea it has positive value.[89]

For Ramos, the contemporary Mexican's sense of inadequacy and inferiority had its roots in the social and historical development of the country. It is the result of a past which he feels he himself had nothing to do with, and therefore is not responsible for its making. On the other hand, Zea firmly believes that the Mexican's responsibility definitely extends to the past. Philosophy, for Zea, involves commitment which

[87] "no ser siempre todavía," p. 213.
[88] *Filosofía sin más*, p. 145.
[89] Villegas, *La filosofía de lo mexicano*, p. 139.

implies responsibility and obligation. Man, in his specific circumstances, by virtue of the fact that he exists, is condemned to act. He is forced to choose between alternatives. He is involved not only in his own existence, but in that of others. His problems and those of his fellow-man are interactive spatially and temporally. This awareness, of necessity, involves the free assumption of one's responsibility for the past. It also commits one to the future. Zea therefore insists that we have to be responsible for a past we have not made, just as we are responsibly involved in a future which will be forged by others. Zea's position thus assumes strong moral overtones: we become a problem for those who have existed in the past to the extent that we represented *their* future in their day, and conceivably determined *their* attitudes.

For a quarter of a century Zea has maintained that the Latin American's supposed inability to philosophize—with the resultant sense of inferiority—is due to a lack of vision vis-à-vis his place in world culture. It is the result of wishing to be someone else, rather than remaining true to oneself. This inferiority feeling is, happily, being replaced by a realization to the effect that the Latin American can achieve whatever is necessary to implement the program which he sets for himself. His sense of maturity should eliminate this feeling of inferiority and make it possible for him to assume responsibilities. This does not mean that he will replace European culture—an equally undesirable posture which would merely demonstrate that he is still motivated by an inferiority complex, by a sense of resentment, rather than by a feeling of confidence and security. He should, therefore, not only continue the work of Western philosophy, but also concentrate on problems that have not been resolved by that philosophy, or with those solutions with which he is dissatisfied. Such problems, dealt with from a Latin American point of view, will necessarily lead to a Latin American philosophy.

Every philosophy has elaborated solutions to similar problems—solutions which are limited by circumstances. The same problems can therefore yield dissimilar solutions. The circumstance in question results in the national character of the philosophy under consideration. Within the Latin American context the problems posed by history require a knowledge of one's past which, in turn, would tend to make for a better adjustment to one's reality and a more effective adaptation of programs to that reality. One who is ignorant of one's history is unable to recognize strengths and weaknesses. He lacks experience, and lack of experience makes for immaturity and, consequently, lack of responsibility.[90]

It is this immaturity which has led Latin America to borrow indiscriminately from the West and to manufacture faulty copies of Euro-

[90] *América como conciencia*, pp. 164-66.

pean doctrines—all of which has been conducive to producing an inauthentic philosophy based on an inauthentic existence.

Confining himself for a moment to the Mexican scene, Zea would have the Mexican begin by assuming responsibilities peculiar to the nation, before concerning himself with world commitments. This has not been done, because of inferiority or irresponsibility. Mexicans have a history, even though it may not be the sort they would like to have made. However, it is their history, their world, one to which only they are answerable.

It is in this connection that Zea criticizes the Peruvian philosopher, Augusto Salazar Bondy, who maintains that an "authentic" philosophy, indeed an authentic existence, is difficult as long as Latin America continues to be an economically underdeveloped continent.

Salazar Bondy complicates the issue by introducing additional terms. Besides "authentic," we must also contend with "peculiar" and "original," and attempt to bear in mind the elements which differentiate one from another. Zea has written that faulty Latin American copies of European philosophy were not necessarily bad; they were simply different. A sense of inferiority was the result of believing that the copy had to be exactly the same as the model (which it can never be). What was really at stake was not so much the copy but the *interpretation* of the model. In short, what was original and peculiar, as this applied to Latin America, was the adaptation.[91] Salazar Bondy is willing to accept this formulation by Zea. He admits that there is a Latin American mode of handling philosophical problems—a sort of cultural hybridization, which merely involves an adaptation of universal philosophical thought to the particular circumstances faced by the continent (p. 95). What he does not admit is that this Latin American philosophic thought is authentic or original. He concedes that it is "peculiar" to the Latin American scene, insofar as this term refers to "the presence of differential historic-cultural traits which lend a distinct character to a spiritual product, in this case, philosophical" (p. 101).

As for the terms "originality" and "authenticity"—as these are applied to the framework of the present discussion—"original," of course, implies a contribution of new ideas, conceptual constructs, and formulations in the truly creative sense; "authentic" refers to a characteristic that flows naturally out of a given set of circumstances, or a product which is inherently part of an organic whole and not derived from an alien body of thought (p. 100). The point made by Salazar Bondy is that a genuine (or authentic) and original Latin American philosophy has not yet been elaborated. There is, however, a philosophy peculiar to Latin America. Some think that the application and interpretation of European ideas result in authenticity; others disagree. A "genuine" or "authentic" quality (the terms are considered

---

[91] Quoted in Salazar Bondy, *¿Existe una filosofía de nuestra América?* p. 93

synonymous) is to be found, for example, in art and literature. The continent is still young from an historical point of view, and philosophy is the product of maturity (p. 104). One might well interject at this point: Does the United States have a philosophy, or at least its own characteristic approach or *Weltanschauung*? It would seem so even though it is at least as old as Latin America.

Salazar Bondy holds that Hispanic American philosophy is defective because of the society of which it is a part. It had originally been imposed by the European conqueror, and subsequently it became the exclusive possession of the ruling class (p. 122). In order to transcend this condition, the Spanish American must emerge from his present circumstances and create new forms of living arrangements. The message is clear: it is necessary to put an end to the present economic underdevelopment and political domination. These have given an air of inauthenticity to the continent. Yet Salazar Bondy seems to contradict himself when he states: "Philosophy in Hispano America, then, has a possibility of being authentic in the midst of the inauthenticity which surrounds and affects it" (pp. 125-26). In order to achieve this, philosophy must reflect upon the anthropological status of the continent, with a view toward its modification. Latin American philosophic thought—placed within the framework of historical challenge—is thus connected intimately with the sort of perspective which confronts the Third World. It cannot be a variation of theoretical concepts which are associated with the present centres of power.

Latin American alienation thus results in philosophical alienation. Alien, inauthentic thought patterns serve to cover up the real Hispanic American reality. They contribute to driving a wedge between what the continent is now and what it was meant to be historically. Therefore, by recognizing the necessity for change and by realizing that this inauthenticity has until now acted as a denial of Hispanic American essence and identity, the new philosophy can assume a positive, constructive role for the entire continent (pp. 131-32).

Zea is quick to counterattack. If, as Salazar Bondy claims, Latin America is still underdeveloped, it would follow that authenticity is a function of development. Yet this is precisely the weakness of Salazar Bondy's argument. Western philosophy, asserts Zea, a product of well-developed, and in some cases, over-developed economies, is itself inauthentic. This is so in view of the fact that it speaks in terms of abstract Man, and negates the individual, specific man; when it extols abstract freedom and acquiesces to the limitations of concrete freedoms for certain peoples; when it sings the praises of democracy, but creates and rationalizes forms of repression which annul the rights of man; and finally, when it justifies the liquidation of human beings in the name of security.[92] One cannot help feeling at this point that Zea has been

---

[92] *Filosofía sin más*, p. 152.

carried away by his own eloquence. Western philosophy has indeed usurped the claim to speak in the name of universal man, as Zea has pointed out on innumerable occasions. But can Zea seriously affirm that *all* of Western philosophy has justified genocide? Nietszche, for example, was utilized and exploited by the Nazis for their nefarious purposes. But one may reasonably doubt whether the German philosopher would have given his approval, had he been alive. Again, in the case of Marxist philosophy, it would be difficult (but not impossible) to make use of this school of thought as a pretext to explain Stalin's bloody rule or terrorist kidnappings and assassinations. And finally, what shall one say of the sad record of man's inhumanity to man in the name of the teachings of the Son of God? History is replete with examples which illustrate the gap that exists between the thinkers, the formulators of theory and doctrine, on the one hand, and the practitioners, the epigones, on the other.

Lack of authenticity, then, in philosophy is not a problem of economic underdevelopment. Developed or over-developed countries of Latin America cannot guarantee authenticity. It is rather a question of man's attitude. Let us not repeat the mistake of thinking that only when we are like Western man in his development will we be like true men in the fullest sense of the word (p. 153).

Authenticity is the result of our capacity to face up to and deal with the problems which confront us, and to work out their solutions. Among these solutions, possibly, is one involving social revolution. But philosophical authenticity is not the *result* of this possible revolution, but rather the *basis* for its possibility. One might well ask here: Is this not too mechanical a formulation? This is akin to saying that an idea is *either* the *cause* or the *effect* of an action that transpires in society. What is missing here is the possibility of admitting a dialectical relationship that may exist between the two elements. They are not mutually exclusive.

Zea coincides with Salazar Bondy when he maintains that philosophy can make Latin America aware of its underdevelopment and indicate possibilities for overcoming this condition. But he insists that authentic philosophy is possible within a climate of inauthenticity. It can act as a beacon and lead the way to correcting this inauthentic situation. There may be more authenticity in past gains or lack thereof in future progress. One must select and separate out the desirable elements. Past attempts which might have been considered "inauthentic" may well turn out to be "authentic." Philosophy might be inauthentic even after Latin America becomes a "developed" continent. In other words, there is no necessary correlation between the two factors. Zea quotes Salazar Bondy to the effect that the new Latin American philosophy, in order to successfully effect a transformation of the status quo, may, at least partially, have to play a destructive role and sweep away myths, idols, and prejudices. One may well ask at this point: Will the new, "authentic" philosophy allow for the substitution of new myths to replace the old? Can man live without myths? The history of the entire present century is living proof that man is not the rational being he so proudly and arrogantly thought he was. In fact, the current developments in literature and the arts demonstrate with painful clarity the minuscule role exercised by man's intellectual prowess, and the power exerted instead by the forces of irrationalism, imagination, and mythology in helping him to adjust to his condition.

In short, the sense of inferiority which has been attributed to the Mexican may also be extended to the rest of Latin America. The continent, too, has experienced an uncomfortable awareness of the "accidental" quality of its culture and essence. Perhaps this is why many Latin American thinkers have always philosophized without being professional philosophers. Philosophy for them was looked upon as a means of "salvation" rather than a "purely theoretical necessity."[93] It was philosophical activity as a function of a concrete reality, yet at the same time an attempt to apply to that reality the results of having dealt with individual themes. It was hoped—and the hope continues to grow—that Latin American originality would emerge as a result of its participation in Western culture, just as European originality can be said to have been the product of the European's solutions to his problems. Yet no conscious Europeanization was intended. True, the Latin American way of life, without being European, involves a life style originally developed in Europe. Or, as the Latin American historian, Edmundo O'Gorman, has put it: "As America goes on being, it stops being America. . . . It annihilates its very essence as it progresses and realizes itself."[94] One notices an interesting dialectical relationship at this point: As this process of "de-Americanization" takes place and Western, i.e., European, life styles are taken over, the latter, simultaneously, cease being exclusively Western, and become universalized—adopted by non-Western countries.

* * * * *

The historicist approach, advanced by Leopoldo Zea to explain the Mexican circumstance, has been criticized by one of his contemporaries, Emilio Uranga, who prefers to attack the problem from an existentialist point of view. Historicism, maintains Uranga, introduces circumstantial impediments which act as a brake upon the intellect. Thought, in Uranga's view, strives to be universal, but is prevented from achieving this quality by these limiting circumstances. Every

[93] Abelardo Villegas, *La filosofía en la historia política de México* (Mexico: Ed. Pormaca, 1966), p. 218.
[94] Quoted in Villegas, *Historia política*, pp. 223-24.

culture has its values, as deserving of study as are those which are presented as models for everyone to emulate. Because historicism has made us aware of our peculiarities, asserts Uranga, we claim the right to live according to our own value system and personality configuration. Nor should we be content with mere analysis of the Mexican essence. We should go beyond that stage and utilize the results of such analysis for the purpose of realizing social, moral, and religious changes within that essence. "We cannot and should not remain the same, both before and after having performed our autognosis."[95]

According to Uranga, the theme of the Mexican is "generational" (in the Orteguian sense). "The Mexican we speak of is the Mexican of our generation . . ." (p. 11). The Mexican has been analyzing himself almost since he was born, historically speaking. "We have been, essentially, an introverted people, in the sense of probing ceaselessly within ourselves" (p. 11). What has changed is that this self-analysis has reached the philosophical plane. It is at this point that the historicist position comes in for criticism, since it is difficult to decide whether history, in and of itself, is sufficient as a methodology to satisfy that which historicism has come to expect.

History, it is said, is the science of the past. But what is really historical is not the past as such, but the specifically human element contained within that past. Since the theme of history is essentially man, it is therefore human and finds its definitive expression in terms of being. Ontological terms, then, are the ultimate to which all other references must be reduced, e.g., history, sociology, psychology, theology, etc. (pp. 14-15).

What we conclude, then, together with Uranga, is that it is entirely erroneous to speak of man as substance, i.e., as finished reality, so dear to the Western philosophical tradition. In fact, all attempts to define man as substantive are inhuman. European man has always been advanced as a model of human dignity, a substantive concept, according to Uranga, and one against which he protests. It was because Mexicans had always felt that they had to emulate this "substance"— and could not—that they proceeded to devaluate themselves. The fact is that human essence is not a finished product; it is, ontologically speaking, an accident. "The inadequacy of the Mexican is simply the insufficiency of his being as an accident" (p. 18). What this means is that he is "unfinished"; nor will he ever be completely "finished." In the same way that sociologists speak of different personality characteristics of the Mexican's "essence," related to regional factors (e.g., rural versus urban, north versus south, etc.), Uranga refers to temporal variations. The Mexican of today is quite different from his compatriot of a century ago. In each case the reality is "open," i.e., the Mexican has to realize himself in accordance with his free will and as an autonomous

[95] *Análisis del ser mexicano*, p. 10.

being. Drawing from Heidegger, Uranga insists that the Mexican, as well as everyone else, is a being who has to be an accident, not a completed substance; he has to realize himself as an accident.

If man is constitutionally accidental, then the Mexican is authentically human. His lack of confidence and sense of inferiority, his vacillation and reluctance to be positive, his hypocrisy, resentment, and cynicism, can now be explained as symptoms which result from his close proximity to the accidental nature of his being. On the other hand, any signs of confidence and generosity, for example, may be viewed as manifestations of his increasing ability to dominate the accidental quality. A greater measure of security can be said to lead him in the direction of substantiality (p. 25).

Applying this concept to the concrete Mexican situation, specifically to the "inferiority" syndrome, it would appear that as far as the Mexican-Spaniard relationship is concerned, the latter represented "substance"; hence, imitation or "malinchismo" was a step toward greater security and less "accidentality."[96] One might well ask in this connection whether, according to the logic dictated by this line of argument, the Mexican feels more "accidental" vis-à-vis the native Indian.

Yet imitation for the purpose of ridding oneself of one's sense of inferiority and the feeling of anxiety that is an inevitable accompaniment are not the solution. The person or group imitated is also "accident," rather than "substance," according to Uranga, since no one, except God, is an absolutely "finished product," i.e., completely realized. The Mexican must come to terms with this fact. He must face uncertainty and "accidentality." This should serve to open his eyes more effectively to the realization of his existential possibilities. We should not allow past wounds to immobilize us, writes Uranga. Perhaps our scars should be re-opened, and old wounds exposed. Only in this way can we rid ourselves of our anxieties and inadequacies, and follow, instead, our original path of self-development—something we never did (p. 148).

One would suppose at this point, in light of the extended discussion of the role played by imitation, that a clearer definition of the terms involved would be forthcoming. Not only is it a question of the kinds of values to be imitated, but also the nature of the process itself. A careful distinction should be made between imitation and assimilation. In the first case, it would seem that the elements in question, i.e., the "native" and the "foreign," remain separate. It is as though the native values were to constitute the base of the chemical liquid; the imitated elements would be found floating on the surface. On the other hand, in the case of assimilation, the two elements would mix and form a new compound.

[96] Uranga, "Ontología del mexicano," p. 147.

* * * * *

Zea has repeatedly asked and attempted to answer his own question: If philosophy is characterized by the universality of the solutions it proposes, how, then, can one speak of a Mexican or a Latin American philosophy, the problems and solutions of which would necessarily be dictated by specifically national or continental circumstances? Zea agrees that philosophy is universal and eternal. But such universality should be the goal striven for by every philosopher. It is not enough to wish to attain a specifically Latin American truth; one must strive to achieve a truth valid for all men, although this may never be realized. Universality is thus limited to the effort, i.e., the striving. The Latin American context cannot be considered as a goal in itself, but rather as a point of departure for a much wider objective. One should, therefore, not attempt to *invent* a Latin American philosophy per se; such an attempt is bound to fail.[97] Instead, as has been said, the aim in Latin America should be to create philosophy, pure and simple. The specifically Latin American texture will eventually emerge and "filter out" in the process as a by-product, a "fringe benefit," so to speak.

One may conceivably discern a contradiction in Zea's formulation. If, as is inevitable, one engages in philosophic discourse by taking cognizance of one's immediate circumstances (one is bound to be affected by their influence), how, then, can one hope—as Zea would like—to attain to a truth which is valid for all men? Zea's own disciple, Abelardo Villegas, places the problem in sharp focus. If, as Zea claims, this universally valid truth is incapable of attainment, then the "Latin American truth" which will emerge as a residue of one's efforts at universality can no longer be considered a "point of departure." Whether we like it or not, it will have to be viewed as an end product.[98]

Yet Zea does not seem concerned. For him this does not represent a contradiction, since he does not think in terms of static, compartmentalized categories. Man does not possess essence, given to him a priori, as traditional philosophy has always maintained. Man is not something already formed; instead, in Orteguian terms, he is a program, he goes on forming himself, evolving continually. Of course, the traditionalist may interject at this point: Yes, he evolves into what he was meant to be eventually, i.e., his essence. Zea would counterattack, saying that the essence of man is precisely his lack of essence. Taking the historicist position, he would argue that generalities have been eliminated, that abstract entities and universal concepts, e.g., "humanity," do not exist. What does exist is a specific set of circumstances which stamp upon man his concrete profile. There are therefore no abstract truths, valid for Man. In fact, the entire concept of humanity was not created by an

[97] See pp. 53-54, 59.
[98] *La filosofía de lo mexicano*, p. 146.

abstract man, but by a concrete individual within a limited circumstance. This same concrete individual has, by virtue of his perspectivism, put an end to universals, and made possible a philosophy of "Mexicanness." What Zea is really saying is that the chain of circumstances is what constitutes history, and it is history which distinguishes the Mexican from other men. But then Zea seems to want it both ways: it is history, too, he claims, which demonstrates that the Mexican has a great deal in common with other human beings. Therein lies the universal quality; the Mexican is human. Truly a case of Scylla and Charybdis!

Since problems are circumstantial, their solutions will be equally so. Contradictions—so runs the argument—appear only when one attempts to convert these solutions into absolutes, applicable to *all* circumstances. A philosophy of "Mexicanness" could therefore fit quite nicely into the framework of historicist relativism. Yet Zea himself wants to go beyond the Mexican circumstance. He wants the Mexican to understand his "essence" by means of capturing the spirit of his past and present; to perceive the characteristics which differentiate him from an Argentine, a Peruvian, a Brazilian, etc. Conversely, what does he share with the rest of Latin America? Or for that matter, what does Latin America have in common with the United States?[99]

As already indicated, Zea affirms that the truths which a given generation lives by are absolute for that generation. "What is not equally absolute is the place which each man or generation occupies in reality" (p. 43). Reality is absolute; points of view, from which this reality can be perceived, are not.

Truths, then, are absolute not in the eternal sense, but only within the context of given circumstances. But are they? May one not argue that truths are also *relative* within that *same* set of circumstances if these are experienced by *different* Mexicans? And will not these truths change if the circumstances change for the *same Mexican?* Yet Zea insists that there are certain truths valuable for all humanity; truths which by the nature of their generality are within the reach of every man. This has to be so; otherwise men could never understand one another.

The trouble seems to be with the definition of the term "circumstance," as Villegas points out. Zea posits the existence of a circumstance so all-inclusive as to be applicable to all of mankind, or in other words, the human circumstance. There are, thus, more inclusive and less inclusive circumstances. (The line of demarcation would be difficult to draw.) Some circumstances are so flexible and so all-embracing as to partake of an absolute quality. They are, therefore, capable of yielding absolute truths. Yet within the framework of circumstantiality, argues Villegas, one cannot affirm the universality of truth. It is incon-

---

[99] *América como conciencia*, p. 24.

sistent to attempt to combine both concepts. "Philosophic truths are either circumstantial or general; they cannot be both at the same time."[100]

The question, of course, is whether a circumstance can be general. Or is it restricted to a condition, limited by time and place? The implication for all those who would like to see a "Mexican" or a "Latin American" philosophy is quite damaging if one is to accept the universality of truth. Villegas suggests that it is not philosophy, but rather history, anthropology, and psychology which are, more properly speaking, the domain for the exploration of Mexican "identity" or "essence." Yet Villegas does not rule out the possibility of philosophizing about the Mexican. But first, one must clear up a key concept: What is meant by "circumstance"? We cannot, on the one hand, say that all truth is circumstantial, and then, when we find ourselves restricted within this apparently rigid pattern, seek a way out by admitting that some truths transcend circumstances.

[100] *La filosofía de lo mexicano*, pp. 151-52.

CONCLUSION

Throughout this study an attempt has been made to capture the "essence," the "personality type," the "national character" of the Mexican, and to place these concepts within the context of Leopoldo Zea's philosophical thought. The terms have been used interchangeably, since several different disciplines have been resorted to in order to view the problem from a variety of perspectives. However, regardless of whether philosophy, sociology, or psychology is appealed to, the fact remains that the Mexican's strengths and weaknesses are a result of his national circumstances. These mould and condition him; they influence the manifold aspects of daily living. In short, history defines man, concrete man, man as a member of a group: what he was, is, and will be. This is central to the thinking of Leopoldo Zea.

Yet somehow, after all the analysis has been performed, one is left with the uneasy feeling that Mexican "essence" is not an undifferentiated entity. "Mexicanness" is not the same for all Mexicans in all parts of the country, or on all levels of society. From a sociological point of view, studies of Mexican character have revealed questionable methodology. For example, data analysis is lacking in many of the studies undertaken. Can one really speak of "the Mexican" in view of the diversity of geographic, socioeconomic, and political components? Do differences between social classes affect this "essence"? Should we not, perhaps, be speaking of "essences" or variations of a given personality configuration?

At the risk of belabouring this point, it is clear that there exists a basic conflict between the philosophical and sociological approaches. The former deals with "essence"; the latter refers to a personality "type." If the two terms are assumed to be synonymous, then one would have to speak in terms of "essences" in order to conform to the sociological framework which makes allowances for "modal types." However, the philosopher may conceivably resist this tendency, and maintain that the same "essence" can also be found in a multiplicity of "types." At best, this difference in perspectives may simply be reduced to an exercise in semantics, since both approaches emphasize certain character traits or qualities in an attempt to define and justify their respective designations.

Mexican sociologists prefer to speak of variability as applied to traits found in different social strata instead of a monolithic personality constellation. "There is no single, definite type, morally, racially, or socially, that can be said to represent the 'Mexican.'"[1]

In this connection, an interesting hypothesis has been advanced, one which makes a distinction between the "Modern Mexican" and the "Pre-Mexican." The former, representing the nucleus of the country's leadership, has acquired a national consciousness and is aware of his responsibility toward other Mexicans. The latter, a cross-section of the population, lacks dynamic aspirations. Both groups evince positive and negative aspects.

For example, there is no sense of national awareness in the Pre-Mexican. He prefers to enjoy the transitory pleasures of the moment, rather than engage in long-range planning. He is irresponsible, a captive of his limitations, yet jealous of the accomplishments of others. However, his stoicism—a positive quality—enables him to suffer his deprivations in silence. On the other hand, the Modern Mexican strives to better himself, as well as work for his country's welfare. He is not representative of a single political group or social class. On the negative side, he represents an element still without technique or structure for unification. What is worse, he proclaims the need for liberating the Pre-Mexican from his state of wretchedness, while continuing to exploit him for personal profit (pp. 179-80).

In the course of this study, also, the danger of falling victim to stereotyped thinking has been ever present. The stereotype, as is well known, represents only a minority of the group under consideration. Certain personality characteristics, subsumed under the philosophical rubric of "essence," such as psychological insecurity, habitual vacillation, feelings of inadequacy, etc., can be found in other ethnic groups which have lived through similar traumatic experiences. How valid, then, is it to say that these other groups possess "Mexican" characteristics?

In other words, is Mexican "inferiority" or "hypersensitivity" an exclusively Mexican characteristic or essence? The temptation to compare Mexican character with other national characters is unavoidable. A comparative approach would necessarily imply that the Mexican is *especially* inferior, as compared with other peoples, that is, if inferiority is to be considered as part of Mexican "essence." In short, a study of Mexican characterology from the comparative point of view, i.e., as compared with other national characters, must be based on the acceptance by all investigators of a general theory of human nature.[2]

And yet, in spite of all the reservations—looking at the reverse side of the coin—it may still be possible, speaking empirically, to prove the existence of certain patterns of behaviour (which may be designated as

[1] Manuel de la Isla Paulín, Epilogue to *Mexican Democracy: A Critical View*, ed. Kenneth F. Johnson (Boston: Allyn and Bacon, 1971), p. 177.
[2] See in this connection Béjar Navarro, p. 176.

"essence"), similar, if not identical, in several *different* groups of Mexicans, regardless of their social status. There are habits, norms, values, and beliefs which may be considered common to all. Hence, to speak in terms of a national character, or of a basic personality structure, is theoretically not only valid, but also possible (pp. 170-71). In this sense, the personality traits under consideration are relatively stable.

Not only is it necessary to ask: What is the Mexican? One must also inquire into the ways in which Mexicans of different social classes function in society, i.e., the interaction between individuals, between groups, and between the individual and the group. Problems involving social status and upward mobility must be examined. What, for example, are the effects of increased industrialization? Can they, possibly, make for a dehumanization of Mexican culture and an accentuation of the various personality traits (e.g., inferiority) discussed in this volume? On the other hand, if the country should not progress materially and industrially, will the consequences be even more undesirable from the standpoint of social relations? For example, González Casanova believes that the poorer the country and the lower the standard of living of the lower classes, the greater the tendency on the part of the higher strata to treat those on the lower rungs of the social ladder as vulgar and inferior by nature. Lower-class humility and courtesy, under these circumstances, may serve as a cover for dangerous frustrations.[3]

A perusal of all the studies of Mexican "character" or "essence" may possibly leave one with the impression that too much emphasis has been placed upon the negative and disagreeable aspects. Certainly an analysis dealing exclusively with anomalies would be far from complete. Yet an examination of this kind—as was pointed out by Samuel Ramos—has always had as its primary objective the development of self-awareness and understanding so that desirable progress might be realized. Perhaps the anomalies discussed by the psychologists and social scientists are not peculiar to the Mexican alone; perhaps the feeling of rootlessness and the fact of marginality would produce similar symptoms in other peoples as well, if these were to find themselves in like circumstances. The Pre-Mexican, referred to above, does not identify with his Indian heritage, nor with the search for national identity. This, then, remains the problem: to attempt to make him part of this identity. The very fact that these personality traits—both positive and negative—can be filtered out for analytical purposes constitutes ample evidence that the so-called Mexican personality is engaged in an ongoing dynamic evolution. Any people, in the process of formation, exhibits subtleties of a similar nature. Any marginal group, buffeted about by conflicting forces, manifests "undesirable" traits, and once made aware of their existence, strives to overcome them, often

---

[3] Pablo González Casanova, *Democracy in Mexico* (New York: Oxford University Press, 1970), p. 181.

oscillating between extremes in the process. For example, contradictory behaviour is illustrated by virtue of the fact that while many
Mexicans refuse to identify with their Indian heritage, there are,
nevertheless, many testimonials to be found in Mexico in honour of
Indian heroes (e.g., Cuauhtemoc). In contrast, no street or monument
bears the name of Cortés, although in recent years there has been some
agitation to correct this situation.

The trouble, then, seems to be that perhaps the Spaniard and the
Indian are still at war with each other within the Mexican psyche. The
much-desired synthesis has not yet been realized. The Mexican is still
not at peace with himself, "his psyche a not yet complete fusion."[4] This
is the tragedy of all marginal peoples who live in a world of complexes,
caused by painful and, at times, irreconcilable contradictions. One
could only hope that the Mexican "personality" would eventually
emerge from this transitional period—if, in fact, this moment can be so
designated—and embark upon the road to a healthier orientation.

In view of all that has been said thus far, it would seem not only
feasible but necessary to carry out studies which deal with the distribution of personality types, as these are found in various subgroups, in
order to ascertain whether a so-called modal personality can be said to
exist. From a sociological point of view—and this would seem to serve
as a counterbalance to philosophical speculation concerning the "essence" of "Mexicanness"—there is need to study with the aid of be-
havioural sciences the *regularity* with which certain personality patterns
are manifested by members of different societies in general, and of
Mexican society in particular.[5] The results of such investigations might
yield valuable insights leading to the determination of what is generally
referred to as a modal or basic personality. This is simply the sum of
peculiarities found to be common or standardized, and which can
justify use of the term "national character." Yet, paradoxically enough,
this national character, as revealed by the structure of the modal
personality, is *not* representative of the *majority* of the group which it
supposedly reflects. If a personality trait, which must be relatively
stable to begin with, is found to exist in fifteen to thirty per cent of the
adult population, then it can be said to constitute a reasonable component of the national character. Five or six such traits are the maximum
number which can be expected to materialize in this proportion.[6] This
is rather disappointing and frustrating, especially for those who wish to
avoid stereotypes which are always based on small percentages. Yet a
stereotype does not always have to be absolutely false. It would help in

---

[4] Victor Alba, *The Mexicans: The Making of a Nation* (New York: Frederick A.
Praeger, 1967), p. 248.

[5] Valuable studies involving national character and personality structure have been
contributed by such noted sociologists and psychologists as Ruth Benedict, Margaret Mead,
Abram Kardiner, Ralph Linton, and Erich Fromm, just to mention a few.

[6] Béjar Navarro, p. 74.

this case if we were to distinguish between a generalization which is supported by evidence, and one which is not. Of course, the question still remains: At what point does one consider the evidence to be "sufficient," especially if one deals in terms of percentages?

Some studies in national character have also distinguished between "social character" and "individual character." Reference has already been made to Erich Fromm,[7] who defines social character "as the nucleus of the character structure which is shared by most members of the same culture,"[8] whereas individual character is that which distinguishes people belonging to the same culture. Social character does not reflect "the sum total of character traits to be found in the majority of people in a given culture."[9] It is, rather, akin to the status occupied by a member of a social group, determined by the function which shapes his energies and makes him behave in a certain way, required by the needs of society. In other words, social character moulds human energy for the purpose of effective functioning. In more developed societies "various classes have a different social character, depending on their different role in the social structure."[10] There can be consonance or disagreement between social and individual character. An individual whose character coincides with his class role tends to become more successful, that is, if economic success is possible. On the other hand, if the economic situation of a class does not provide for such a possibility, then only that individual whose character differs from the social character of his class can escape from his level of poverty.[11]

Character, then, or "essence," is closely related to social structure. The behaviour of the individual is conditioned by his position, role, and function within each of the social institutions wherein he operates. To complicate matters even further, these institutions themselves undergo change. They may be static or dynamic; they may have varying degrees of cohesion or they may disintegrate. All of this takes place within the context of "culture," which is the historic result of human interaction and includes ideas, values, and norms. Norms place individuals in certain categories, thus making for social differentiation or stratification. The character structure is thereby inferred from the individual's actions which may be habitual or meaningful, and are the result of his patterns of motivations and attitudes.

Within the terms of this psychosociological framework one may well ask: does it not become somewhat difficult to engage in philosophical speculation about a Mexican essence, even if one were to

[7] See Preface, p. xii.
[8] Fromm, "Psychoanalytical Characterology and its Application to the Understanding of Culture," p. 4.
[9] Ibid.
[10] Fromm and Maccoby, p. 17. Ralph Linton prefers the term "status personality." See his "Problems of Status Personality," in *Culture and Personality*, ed. S. Stansfield Sargent and Marion W. Smith (New York: Viking Fund, 1949), p. 66.
[11] Fromm and Maccoby, p. 230.

allow for, or even insist upon, the possibility of change, to be experienced by this "essence"?[12] For no one has as yet argued in favour of the "unchangeability" of Mexican essence. Uranga, for example, speaks of the "accidental," uncertain quality of the Mexican. If "accidence" is a constant factor, is it, therefore, peculiarly "Mexican"? The truth is that *man* himself, the world over, is accidental. One cannot speak—as Uranga seems to be doing—of the Mexican as though he were an entity entirely removed from all time, as well as from the sociopolitical context.[13] Not only does the Mexican function in time and space—a fact which might have produced his resentment, his attitude toward death, and all the other traits supposedly monopolized by him. These very same traits are also evident in other parts of the world, and are experienced by people who have, similarly, been victims of their own unstable circumstances. Nor is there any law which decrees that all individuals who have experienced instability must turn out to be "resentful," "inferior," "envious," etc. Like causes do not always produce like results. Parenthetically, unlike causes may yield similar results. José Revueltas asks with good reason: Who is the real Mexican? Which of the following represents authentic Mexicanness: the lower-class city dweller who is a hypocrite and a sexual sadist; the intellectual who is tortured by vanity, twisted and envious, and full of obscure repressions; the inhabitant of Monterrey or Lower California who is calm, sober, and cordial?[14]

Again, in the philosophical sense, is it correct to speak about Mexicanness in the first place? Is it valid to be concerned with the "nature" of the Mexican insofar as this is related to the development of ideas? Is Mexican "character," "reality," or "essence" a necessary ingredient to be contained in a philosophy which is created by Mexican thinkers? Is it a prerequisite, a conditioning agent, or a by-product? Or possibly all three? What does Mexicanness actually consist of from a philosophical point of view? What are the "peculiarities" which distinguish the Mexican from the so-called "universal man," that is, if the latter can be said to exist?

We have seen that Leopoldo Zea has attempted to wrestle with this problem and with the difficulties involved. In all fairness, it should be

[12] See above, p. 121.

[13] Uranga, in fact, has been charged with inconsistency. In his excellent critique, Martin Stabb points to the contradiction: Uranga's conceptual structures which describe reality may have a universal quality about them, yet Uranga himself stresses the circumstantiality of his position. Moreover, there is a certain static quality about Uranga's "ontology": it implies "being," rather than "becoming." In spite of this, Uranga would have the Mexican "complete" his structure. What specifically, asks Stabb, can Uranga add to Mexican character in order to bring about the desired moral, social, and religious transformation? (Martin Stabb, *In Quest of Identity* [Chapel Hill: University of North Carolina Press, 1967], pp. 213-14.)

[14] José Revueltas, "Posibilidades y limitaciones del mexicano," *Filosofía y Letras* 20, no. 40 (October-December 1950), 260.

pointed out again that Zea does not consider Mexican essence the alpha and omega of his line of thought. The Mexican circumstance and the "essence" it has produced are just a point of departure. Zea proceeds in ever-widening concentric circles. Man is an historical entity, which means that his essence is change. The Mexican is no exception. He, too, is both the subject and object of history which has moulded his essence or being. But Zea does not stop with Mexican history. He situates it within the context of American history, and subsequently places American history within the framework of universal history. By doing so, he makes the Mexican a part of humankind. This is equivalent to taking stock of one's own human self, and, finally, of the essential humanity of others. Only by linking the national to the international does Zea succeed in joining the Mexican with the rest of humanity.

Yet the desire to broaden one's horizons has its dangers. The Mexican, and, by extension, the Latin American, has mistakenly imitated the products of Western culture. What he should do, instead, according to Zea, is to emulate the spirit and attitude of the West, i.e., he should develop the capacity to face up to difficulties rather than avoid them, and find adequate solutions to the problems which present themselves. Only by cultivating this spirit can he lay claim to any degree of originality and authenticity. This is the task which Latin American philosophers should set for themselves. This will constitute their contribution.

* * * * *

Ortega's influence upon Zea's thinking is unmistakable. Man—any man—without a program lacks authenticity. If he does not utilize his possibilities to realize himself, he degenerates into a mere thing. He loses his humanity because he has no direction. This is a clear example of the relationship which history, according to Zea, bears to philosophy. For man is capable of perceiving just what it is that history imposes upon him, and what he, in turn, can impose upon his environment. History thus becomes "the realization of the essence of man."[15] Moreover, for Zea the historian's task is to "point out spiritual directions, collective projects and ideas which order, according to our purposes, the historical process of a nation."[16] This approach can be said to complement the existentialist perspective which holds that historiography, generally speaking, is a matter of making the past adequate for the needs of the present. Of course, this point of view stands in sharp contrast to so-called "objective" or "external" history, which attempts to eliminate subjective bias. Such objectivity, which

[15] Rippy, p. 226.
[16] Luis Villoro, "The Historian's Task: The Mexican Perspective," *The New World Looks at its History*, ed. A. R. Lewis and T. F. McGann (Austin: The University of Texas Press, 1963), p. 179.

strives to present bare facts "scientifically," is next to impossible. The facts themselves are merely symbols of cultural changes, and represent reflections of the human spirit. Historiography of this type, undeniably romantic in origin and scope, is primarily concerned with meaning, rather than bare description and recording. It is at this point that philosophy and history touch each other and give birth to the history of ideas, which attempts to shed light on human attitudes and motivations. "As man invents historical entities in his own image and likeness," writes Edmundo O'Gorman, "knowing them we come to know their inventor."[17] The past is made adequate in order to satisfy the exigencies of the present. The danger which results from this type of historiography needs no comment. Re-writing history, a consequence of "revisionism," leads easily to distortion and falsification. However, this does not seem to bother some of the foremost exponents of this approach. "Even within the same culture each generation yearns for and constructs an image of the past in accordance with its preoccupations and its mentality, and for that reason the image always differs from that of the preceding generation."[18]

Historians who had recorded facts "objectively" (e.g., the Positivists) in an attempt to eliminate subjective bias, had apparently divorced the past from the present. They had lost sight of the need to give direction to the present, and had forgotten that historical "facts" had meaning for the future. What must be borne in mind is that collective human attitudes are more important than "objective" events devoid of meaning. What is imperative is a "clarification of significant structures that transcend the sum of bare facts."[19]

Historicists and existentialist historians view "objective" or "positivist" historiography as pure illusion. Even the "scientific" historian, conditioned as he is by his own circumstances, cannot escape injecting, even subconsciously, value judgments and cultural bias. What is obvious here is that sociological "objectivity" and philosophical romanticism have met on the battlefield of history and are engaged in combat. The active, creative principle, which is more interested in future-oriented purposes than in static products of the past, is typical of Zea and others like him, and has determined his choice of options.

* * * * *

Zea is perfectly aware that existentialism does not solve problems; it poses them. It is an attitude, rather than a system, and forces man to come to grips with his reality.[20] Latin American philosophy, Zea feels,

---

[17] Edmundo O'Gorman, "Classical or Ontological History," in ibid., pp. 203-204.
[18] Guillermo Céspedes del Castillo, "The 'Mestizo' Quality in Current Historiography," in ibid., p. 206.
[19] Villoro, "Historian's Task," p. 179.
[20] *La filosofía como compromiso*, p. 170.

must transcend its particular circumstances. If it broadens its horizons in the process of dealing with problems affecting humanity, it will realize that it, too, is human—a quality which has been denied it by the Western World. Zea has fought consistently against that distorted concept of "universality," advocated by Europeans—distorted because the latter view as unimportant any cultural manifestation that does not originate in western Europe.

Yet lest this attitude give way to any misinterpretation, Zea is not opposed to universality per se. "Philosophy is not satisfied with the attainment of circumstantial truth; instead, it strives to arrive at universal truth."[21] Nevertheless, circumstantial factors determine truths, according to which each generation governs itself. If this should appear to be a contradictory position—i.e., to posit resistance to "particularity" and defence of "circumstantiality" at the same time—Zea is quick to extricate himself from the dilemma. Even though the various truths or points of view are not absolute, reality itself is. Hence, each point of view represents an absolute value for the particular generation which harbours it. Only then can it be said, perhaps, that Latin America will have come of age. But the philosophy that will emerge must not—as Patrick Romanell has indicated—deny cultural relations with other parts of the world, especially with Europe. It must be an American, not an "Americanist" philosophy.[22] It cannot degenerate into Narcissism or chauvinism.

Philosophy in Mexico, then, and in Latin America, generally, is based on that which is peculiar to Latin America. What does the Mexican have in common with other peoples? What is different about him? Perhaps the answer to the latter question and the solutions to problems this entails can be offered to others who are faced with similar circumstances.

If, within the present context, one were to accept Marx's dictum that it is not enough to interpret the world, but that one must also change it, then one would be compelled to agree with Samuel Ramos. For Ramos opened the door to those who subsequently engaged in the task of analyzing the Mexican, and proceeded to outline the responsibility of the Latin American philosopher. Philosophy, for this school of thought—especially from the Latin American point of view—should not limit itself to formulating, interpreting, and presenting a conception of the world and of men therein. It should also be a means of defining the Latin American circumstance, and an instrumentality for transforming the relationship which the inhabitant of this continent bears to the rest of the world. The point to remember, too, is that ideas in Latin America have always tended to be weapons, utilized in the

[21] *Filosofía americana*, p. 32.
[22] Patrick Romanell, *La formación de la mentalidad mexicana* (Mexico: El Colegio de México, 1954), p. 174.

never-ending confrontation with reality. Many Latin American philosophers have, therefore, been considered ideologues, intent upon resolving problems. The urgency of the circumstances did not allow for time to create original systems. Zea, referred to by Romanell as the "Ramos of the present generation" (p. 166), has always felt that great philosophers of history have also been possessed by the urge to improve and reform. Even after having engaged in the most abstract of metaphysical questions, they always returned to social and political reality in order to change it. Leopoldo Zea, too, has adhered to the tenets of this great tradition.

EPILOGUE

As this study was going to press, Leopoldo Zea published yet another volume,[1] a synthesis, it would appear, of all his earlier works.[2] The strands of previous themes are tied together, and the main thrust of Zea's several decades of philosophic and historical writing is brought into sharper focus and given more elaborate detail.

The central theme in the history of ideas, propounded by Zea, continues to be the marginality and dependence of Latin American thought upon European or Western intellectual development. The latter is an outgrowth of the cultural scene which gave it sustenance, i.e., Western philosophical thought evolved as a result of the interplay of social forces which characterized the history of its environment. According to Zea, it has successfully absorbed and assimilated various and often contradictory elements, a point which may be argued. However, this has not been the case with Latin America. The history of ideas, as this relates to the Latin American scene, has been marked by a borrowing and an appropriation of foreign concepts—European in origin—which have supposedly been alien to the native (i.e., Latin American), historical context. Such concepts might well have been in accord with European reality but not with the Latin American scene. The situation becomes all the more acute in view of the desire of Latin Americans to utilize models of European and Western thought for the purpose of altering their own reality. The implication is quite clear, an implication which Zea resists: the models to be followed are representative of a supposedly superior culture. The Latin American pattern is obviously inferior if it has to be improved.

European history, then, is one of absorption by means of synthesis, while that of Latin America is merely a collection of unassimilable, often conflicting elements. Latin America has accumulated problems, not solutions (p. 20). In this respect, it is no different from any other dependent or marginal country. The philosophy characteristic of these subordinate groups is perforce unlike that of imperial and colonizing nations. Zea thus links the history of ideas, and the philosophy of history in particular, with the political and economic status of a people. The philosophy of history of Latin America cannot be content with a

[1] Leopoldo Zea, *Filosofía de la historia americana* (Mexico: Fondo de Cultura Económica, 1978).

[2] In a personal chat with the writer, in Mexico City, in December 1978, Zea implied that he "has said it all."

mere acceptance of the status quo. Passive awareness is not enough. By contrast, a knowledge of facts in order to change these facts, if need be, becomes the central task of a Latin American philosophy of history. Summing up, this involves the inevitable dialectic of stimulus and response with the Western World.

The history of ideas of Latin America has always been viewed from a European or Western-oriented point of view. Philosophic structures had been adopted to fit a Latin American reality. It was Europe that had given meaning to the Latin American historical phenomenon. But now this view needs to be changed. It is necessary for Latin America to take a look at Europe and the Western World, and to judge accordingly. The vision of the vanquished, the dominated, and the colonized will now determine the sense of Latin American history. To put it succinctly: the monologue of the colonizers has to be replaced by the dialogue between the expanding nations and the dependent areas of the world (p. 28). History is not just the expression of dominant powers. The moment has arrived for objects to transform themselves into subjects—and this, not exclusively for Latin America.[3] The transformation affects the entire Third World as well.

However, outright rejection of European-inspired patterns of thought and behaviour is not sufficient. Zea emphasizes an oft-repeated theme: the rejection by Latin America, which should be a dialectical negation, is achieved by utilizing, not imitating blindly, the European models of the past in the service of more optimistic goals of the future.

The interpretation of universal history, claims Zea, has been European-slanted, simply because the philosophy of history, as a philosophical discipline, appeared at a moment when Europe had penetrated all parts of the globe through its expansionist policies. The European, taking stock of himself and his exploits, sought a philosophic justification for all that he had accomplished and was yet to achieve. He saw himself as one who had triumphed over the forces of nature, who had harnessed and channelled them to his purposes. Hegel had asserted that history was the record of man's efforts to liberate himself from the bonds of slavery and, in the process, to gain increasing control of nature's domain. Unfortunately, nature consisted not only of territory, flora and fauna, but also of human beings who inhabited other, non-European parts of the globe. These had not entered into Hegel's calculations; these were marginal because they

[3] How does an "object" become a "subject"? By wielding economic power, for example. Mexico's newly discovered oil deposits may yet contribute to diminishing the sense of "inferiority" experienced by the Mexican psyche vis-à-vis the United States. President Carter's visit to Mexico for the purpose of obtaining oil imports for his country illustrates the case admirably. The change in tone and attitude of the Mexican President in addressing his American counterpart may signal a shift in the relationship between the two countries.

had not followed the European pattern. It remained for Marx and Engels, according to Zea, to correct this perspective, this "oversight"—a correction, ironically enough, which had also originated in European thought, to be adopted subsequently by non-European peoples. A correction which involved the humanization of man, including all those groups which had remained at the periphery of Hegel's perspective.

Within this framework the Iberian expansionism of the sixteenth century was to be challenged three centuries later by what Zea calls the "libertarian project" of the Latin Americans. However, in the process of liberating themselves, the Latin Americans imitated the model of the more "modern" and "civilizing" European influences—as opposed to the older Iberian-Catholic perspective—in such a manner as to result in a new form of dependency. Adopting the new model as their own led them to a policy of self-denigration and a deprecation of their own value system. This, Zea feels, must be corrected. Latin America must free itself of its dependence and recover its own reality, by recognizing and overcoming the errors derived from its conservative Iberian past, as well as those of the more recent European expansionism.

Latin America is a concrete illustration of the dilemma caused by two apparently competing philosophical orientations: freedom versus equality. But only apparently, since they are not really contradictory but rather complementary (p. 39). The less favoured nations of the world are more interested in equality—and this, in a material sense—than in freedom, considered from a moral or legal point of view. The fact is that economic inequality is an obstacle to the possibility of attaining and enjoying such freedom. Freedom is not only that which is exercised by man in his confrontation with and mastery of nature; it is, rather, a concept which involves men or people in their relationships with other men and peoples. In this context, freedom exercised by certain nations has only resulted in greater inequalities for other nations. The United States, for example, was born in freedom; its basic philosophy in the course of its development has been libertarian. Latin America would very much like to adopt this policy as its own. The problem is that it cannot, because it is not economically equal to the United States. Moreover, these economic inequalities are the very result of the libertarian ideals of the United States and the rest of the Western World. What it all really amounts to is that this is no longer a conflict between ideals and philosophies, but between material interests. If the United States, as leader of the West, were to be faced with the necessity of having to surrender some of its economic gains in order to effect a more equitable distribution of material wealth among the disadvantaged nations of the world—a redistribution which would enable these nations to realize a greater measure of freedom—then, maintains Zea, the United States, as well as the rest of the Western World, would be ready to jettison that freedom. "To the devil with freedom, but with the freedom of other peoples" (p. 42). In short, the principle of freedom seems to have been utilized by the West, especially by its principal spokesman, the United States, to enrich itself, and even to intervene in the affairs of others in order to perpetuate that same principle. Ironically, such intervention is realized while the right of self-determination is proclaimed for the very nation in which the intervention takes place, and "freedom" is thereby protected.

A philosophy of Latin American history within this framework, concludes Zea, becomes a philosophy which recognizes the role of dependence upon the West by the rest of the world, and the consequent struggle for freedom from such dependence. Such a philosophy will also stress the fact that freedom depends for its realization on the recognition of another, equally important principle, namely, a greater measure of economic well-being for all racial, religious, and national cultures. Yesterday Latin America confronted Spain and Western Europe in its struggle for freedom and equality. Today the adversary is the United States.

In the context of Zea's formulation of the problem, one would have to arrive at a rather melancholy, yet far from novel, conclusion. If man's ingenuity is not sufficiently resourceful to make possible the increase and improvement of the world's storehouse of material riches, then the great majority of humankind, inhabiting the more disadvantaged portions of the globe, is heading on a collision course with those nations which have hitherto occupied the more favoured status in society.

There will undoubtedly be periods of adjustments and compromise, shifting alliances between nations and between diverse groups within a given nation, in order to attempt to avoid a potential cataclysm. Yet if one is to judge from past history, the outlook is not overly optimistic. There is no greater indictment of human intelligence than the thought contained in the popular adage, "history repeats itself." For this implies that we learn very little; we do not profit from past mistakes. If we did, history would *not* repeat itself. Military clashes due to conflicts of economic interests are rapidly reaching the point of no return, given the advanced state of technology developed for the purpose of annihilating humankind. A global Armageddon, produced by a nuclear holocaust, should make influential groups of all nations—both the "haves" and the "have nots"—pause and revise their thinking as they pursue their respective programs for the implementation of freedom and equality.

SELECTED BIBLIOGRAPHY

Alba, Victor. *The Mexicans: The Making of a Nation*. New York: Frederick A. Praeger, 1967.

Altamirano, Isaías. "El sentido mexicano del tiempo." *Filosofía y Letras* (Mexico) 21, nos. 41-42 (January-June 1951).

Ardao, Arturo. "Un enfoque mexicano del positivismo uruguayo." *Marcha* (Montevideo, Uruguay), December 30, 1949.

Arévalo, Juan J. *Fábula del tiburón y las sardinas*. Buenos Aires: Editorial Palestra, 1961.

Basave Fernández del Valle, Agustín. *Samuel Ramos*. Mexico: Universidad de Nuevo León, 1965.

Batt, Carl E. "Mexican Character: An Adlerian Interpretation." *Journal of Individual Psychology* 25, no. 2 (November 1969).

Béjar Navarro, Raúl. *El mito del mexicano*. 2nd ed., Mexico: Editorial Orientación, 1971.

Bermúdez, María Elvira. *La vida familiar del mexicano*. Mexico: Porrúa y Obregón, 1955.

Carrión, Jorge. "Ciencia y magia del mexicano." *Cuadernos Americanos* (Mexico) 2 (1948).

————. *Mito y magia del mexicano*. 3rd ed., Mexico: Porrúa y Obregón, 1971.

Caso, Alfonso. *El pueblo del sol*. Colección Popular. Mexico: Fondo de Cultura Económica, 1971.

Caso, Antonio. *México, apuntamientos de cultura patria*. Mexico: Imprenta Universitaria, 1943.

Céspedes del Castillo, Guillermo. "The 'Mestizo' Quality in Current Historiography." In *The New World Looks at its History*. Edited by A. R. Lewis and T. F. McGann. Austin: The University of Texas Press, 1963.

Cosío Villegas, Daniel. *Extremos de América*. Mexico: Fondo de Cultura Económica, 1949.

Fanon, Franz. *The Wretched of the Earth*. New York: Grove Press, 1963.

FitzHugh, David. "Whatever Happened to the New Dialogue with Latin America?" *Saturday Review*, October 18, 1975.

Fromm, Erich. "Psychoanalytic Characterology and its Application to the Understanding of Culture." In *Culture and Personality*. Edited by S. Stansfield Sargent and Marion W. Smith. New York: Viking Fund, 1949.

————. and Maccoby, Michael. *Social Character in a Mexican Village*. Englewood Cliffs, N.J.: Prentice-Hall, 1970.

Fuentes, Carlos. *La región más transparente*. Mexico: Fondo de Cultura Económica, 1968.

Gamio, Manuel. *Forjando patria*. Mexico: Librería de Porrúa Hermanos, 1916.

Gaos, José. *Filosofía mexicana de nuestros días*. Mexico: Imprenta Universitaria, 1954.

————. *El pensamiento hispanoamericano*. Mexico: El Colegio de México, 1943.

_____. *En torno a la filosofía mexicana.* Vol. 2. Mexico: Porrúa y Obregón, 1955.
García Ruiz, Alfonso. "El positivismo en México." *Revista de Historia de América* (Mexico: El Colegio de México) 16 (December 1943).
Garizurieta, César. *Isagoge sobre lo mexicano.* Mexico: Porrúa y Obregón, 1952.
Gómez Robleda, José. *Psicología del mexicano.* Mexico: Universidad Nacional Autonoma de Mexico, 1962.
González Casanova, Pablo. *Democracy in Mexico.* New York: Oxford University Press, 1970.
_____. "*La estructura social y cultural de México* by José Iturriaga." *Filosofía y Letras* (Mexico) 22, nos. 43-44 (July-December 1951).
González Pineda, Francisco. *El Mexicano: psicología de su destructividad.* 6th ed., Ed. Pax-Mexico, 1972.
_____. *El Mexicano: su dinámica psicosocial.* 4th ed., Ed. Pax-Mexico, 1971.
Gorer, Geoffrey. *The American People.* New York: W. W. Norton, 1948.
Griffin, Charles C. "*América en la historia* by Leopoldo Zea." *American Historical Review* 58 (April 1958).
Hale, Charles A. "Substancia y método en el pensamiento de Leopoldo Zea." *Historia Mexicana* (Mexico: El Colegio de México) 20, no. 2 (October-December 1970).
Halperin, Maurice. *The Rise and Decline of Fidel Castro.* Berkeley: University of California Press, 1972.
Hamady, Sania. *Temperament and Character of the Arabs.* New York: Twayne Publishers, 1960.
Hernández Luna, Juan. "Primeros estudios sobre el mexicano en nuestro siglo." *Filosofía y Letras* (Mexico) 20, no. 4 (October-December 1950).
_____. *Samuel Ramos: su filosofía sobre lo mexicano.* Mexico: UNAM, 1956.
de la Isla Paulín, Manuel. Epilogue to *Mexican Democracy: A Critical View.* Edited by Kenneth F. Johnson. Boston: Allyn and Bacon, 1971.
Iturriaga, José E. *La estructura social y cultural de México.* Mexico: Fondo de Cultura Económica, 1951.
Knockenhauer, María de los Angeles. "José Gaos y la filosofía de lo mexicano." *Revista de la Universidad de México* 24, no. 9 (May 1970).
Lewis, A. R. and McGann, T. F. *The New World Looks at its History.* Austin: The University of Texas Press, 1963.
Lewis, Oscar. *Five Families.* New York: Science Editions, 1962.
Linton, Ralph. "Problems of Status Personality." In *Culture and Personality.* Edited by S. Stansfield Sargent and Marion W. Smith. New York: Viking Fund, 1949.
Maciel, D. and Padilla, A. "The National Character of Mexico: Myth or Reality?" *Proceedings of the Pacific Coast Council on Latin American Studies* 3 (San Diego: San Diego State University, 1974).
Maccoby, Michael. "Love and Authority: A Study of Mexican Villagers." *The Atlantic* 213, no. 3 (1964).
Madariaga, Salvador de. *Englishmen, Frenchmen and Spaniards: An Essay in Comparative Psychology.* London: Oxford University Press, 1928.
Mannheim, Karl. *Ideology and Utopia.* New York: Harcourt, Brace & Co., 1946.
Mayz Vallenilla, Ernesto. "El problema de América." In *Antología de la filosofía americana contemporánea.* Edited by Leopoldo Zea. Mexico: B. Costa-Amic, 1968.
Murena, H. A. *El pecado original de América.* Buenos Aires: Ed. Sudamericana, 1965.
Nicol, Eduardo. "Meditación del propio ser." *Filosofía y Letras* (Mexico) 20, no. 4 (October-December 1950).

Northrop, F. S. C. *The Meeting of East and West.* New York: Macmillan, 1946.

O'Gorman, Edmundo. "Classical or Ontological History." In *The New World Looks at its History.* Edited by A. R. Lewis and T. F. McGann. Austin, 1963.

Paz, Octavio. *El laberinto de la soledad.* 3rd ed., Mexico: Fondo de Cultura Económica, 1963.

Phelan, John Leddy. "México y lo mexicano." *The Hispanic American Historical Review* 36, no. 3 (August 1956).

Picón-Salas, Mariano. *De la conquista a la Independencia.* Mexico: Fondo de Cultura Económica, 1944.

Raat, William D. "Ideas e historia en México: un ensayo sobre metodología." In *Latino América, Anuario, Estudios Latinoamericanos, No. 3.* Mexico: Universidad Nacional Autónoma de México, 1970.

——————. "Leopoldo Zea and Mexican Positivism: A Reappraisal." *The Hispanic American Historical Review* 48, no. 1 (February 1968).

Rama, Angel. "Un filósofo examina América Latina." *Marcha* (Montevideo), September 1964.

Ramírez, Santiago. *El mexicano: Psicología de sus motivaciones.* 8th ed., Mexico: Editorial Pax, 1972.

Ramos, Samuel. *El perfil del hombre y la cultura en México.* 5th ed., Mexico: Austral, 1972.

——————. "En torno a las ideas sobre el mexicano." *Cuadernos Americanos* (Mexico) 57, no. 3 (May-June 1951).

Revueltas, Eugenia. "José Gaos y la circunstancia literaria." *Revista de la Universidad de México* 24, no. 9 (May 1970).

Revueltas, José. "Posibilidades y limitaciones del mexicano." *Filosofía y Letras* (Mexico) 20, no. 40 (October-December 1950).

Reyes, Alfonso. *La x en la frente.* Mexico: Porrúa y Obregón, 1952.

——————. "Notas sobre la inteligencia americana." In *Ultima Tule.* In *Obras completas* 11 (Mexico: Fondo de Cultura Económica, 1960).

Reyes Nevárez, Salvador. *El amor y la amistad en el mexicano.* Mexico: Porrúa y Obregón, 1962.

Rippy, Merrill. "Theory of History: Twelve Mexicans." *The Americas* 17, no. 3 (January 1961).

Romanell, Patrick. *La formación de la mentalidad mexicana.* Mexico: El Colegio de México, 1954.

——————. "Samuel Ramos on the Philosophy of Mexican Culture: Ortega and Unamuno in Mexico." *Latin American Research Review* 10, no. 3 (Fall 1975).

Romero, Francisco. "El americanismo filosófico de Leopoldo Zea." *La Prensa* (Buenos Aires), July 27, 1958.

Salazar Bondy, Augusto. *¿ Existe una filosofía de nuestra América?* Mexico: Siglo XXI Editores, 1968.

Salazar Mallén, Rubén. *Samuel Ramos.* Mexico: Secretaría de Educación Pública, 1968.

Sargent, S. S. and Smith, M. W. *Culture and Personality.* New York: Viking Fund, 1949.

Segura Millán, Jorge. *Diorama de los mexicanos.* Mexico: B. Costa-Amic, 1964.

Stabb, Martin S. *In Quest of Identity.* Chapel Hill: University of North Carolina Press, 1967.

Stavenhagen, Rodolfo. *Las clases sociales en las sociedades agrarias.* Mexico: Siglo XXI, 1969.

Stein, Stanley, J. "Review of *The Latin American Mind*," a translation of Zea's *Dos etapas del pensamiento en Hispanoamérica* by James B. Abbott and Lowell

Dunham (Norman: University of Oklahoma Press, 1963). In *Political Science Quarterly* 80 (March 1965).

Stonequist, E. V. *The Marginal Man: A Study in Personality and Culture Conflict.* New York: Charles Scribner's Sons, 1937.

Toynbee, Arnold. "Making Greed Look Respectable." *The Montreal Star*, January 26, 1974.

_____ . *México y el occidente.* Mexico: Antigua Librería Robredo, 1956.

Uranga, Emilio. *Análisis del ser del mexicano.* Mexico: Porrúa y Obregón, 1952.

_____ . "Ensayo de una ontología del mexicano." *Cuadernos Americanos* (Mexico) 54, no. 2 (March-April 1949).

_____ . "Notas para un estudio del mexicano." *Cuadernos Americanos* 57, no. 3 (May-June 1951).

_____ . "Optimismo y pesimismo del mexicano." In *Historia Mexicana* 1 (1951).

Usigli, Rodolfo. "Epílogo sobre la hipocresía del mexicano" (1938). In *El Gesticulador.* Mexico: Editorial Stylo, 1947.

Vasconcelos, José. *Etica.* Madrid: Aguilar, 1932.

Villegas, Abelardo. "José Gaos y la filosofía hisponoamericana." *Revista de la Universidad de México* 24, no. 9 (May 1970).

_____ . *La filosofía de lo mexicano.* Mexico: Fondo de Cultura Económica, 1960.

_____ . *La filosofía en la historia política de México.* Mexico: Ed. Pormaca, 1966.

Villoro, Luis. "Historia de las ideas." *Historia Mexicana* 15 (1965-1966).

_____ . "The Historian's Task: The Mexican Perspective." In *The New World Looks at its History.* Edited by A. R. Lewis and T. F. McGann. Austin: The University of Texas Press, 1963.

Zum Felde, Alberto. *El problema de la cultura americana.* Buenos Aires: Editorial Losada, 1943.

Works by Leopoldo Zea

Books

Zea, Leopoldo. *América como conciencia.* Mexico: Cuadernos Americanos, 1953.

_____ . *América en la conciencia de Europa.* Mexico: Los Presentes, 1955.

_____ . *América en la historia.* Mexico: Fondo de Cultura Económica, 1957.

_____ . *Antología del pensamiento social y políitico de América Latina.* Washington, D.C.: Unión Panamericana, 1964.

_____ . *Antología de la filosofíia americana contemporánea.* Mexico: B. Costa-Amic, 1968.

_____ . *Apogeo y decadencia del positivismo en México.* Mexico: El Colegio de México, 1944.

_____ . *Conciencia y posibilidad del mexicano.* Mexico: Porrúa y Obregón, 1952.

_____ . *Dependencia y liberación en la cultura latinoamericana.* Mexico: Editorial Joaquín Mortiz, 1974.

_____ . *Dialéctica de la conciencia americana.* Mexico: Alianza Editorial Mexicana, 1976.

_____ . *Dos etapas del pensamiento en Hispanoamérica.* Mexico: El Colegio de México, 1949.

_____ . *Ensayos sobre filosofía en la historia.* Mexico: Ed. Stylo, 1948.

_____ . *En torno a una filosofía americana.* Mexico: El Colegio de México, 1945.

_____ . *La esencia de lo americano.* Buenos Aires: Editorial Pleamar, 1971.
_____ . *Esquema para una historia de las ideas en Iberoamérica.* Mexico: Imprenta Universitaria, 1956.
_____ . *Esquema para una historia del pensamiento en México.* Lima, 1946.
_____ . *Filosofía de la historia americana.* Mexico: Fondo de Cultura Económica, 1978.
_____ . *La filosofía americana como filosofía sin más.* Mexico: Siglo XXI, Editores, S.A., 1969.
_____ . *La filosofía como compromiso.* Mexico: Tezontle, 1952.
_____ . *Introducción a la filosofía.* 3rd ed., Mexico: Imprenta Universitaria, 1967.
_____ . *Latinoamérica: Emancipación y neocolonialismo.* Caracas: Editorial Tiempo Nuevo, 1971.
_____ . *Latinoamérica en la formación de nuestro tiempo.* Mexico: Cuadernos Americanos, 1965.
_____ . *Latinoamérica: Tercer Mundo.* Mexico: Editorial Extemporáneos, 1977.
_____ . *Latinoamérica y el mundo.* Caracas: Universidad Central de Venezuela, 1950.
_____ . *Latin America and the World.* Trans. by F. K. Hendricks and B. Berler. Norman: University of Oklahoma Press, 1969.
_____ . *The Latin American Mind.* A translation of *Dos etapas del pensamiento en Hispanoamérica*, by J. R. Abbott and L. Dunham. Norman: University of Oklahoma Press, 1960.
_____ et al. *Major Trends in Mexican Philosophy.* Chicago: University of Notre Dame Press, 1966.
_____ . *El occidente y la conciencia de México.* Mexico: Porrúa y Obregón, 1953.
_____ . *El Pensamiento Latinoamericano.* 2 vols. Mexico: Ed. Pormaca, 1965.
_____ . *El positivismo en México.* 1st ed. Mexico: El Colegio de México, 1943.
_____ . *El positivismo en México—Nacimiento, apogeo y decadencia.* 2nd ed. Mexico: Fondo de Cultura Económica, 1968.
_____ , ed. *Los Precursores del pensamiento latinoamericano contemporáneo.* Mexico: Secretaría de la Educación Pública, 1971.

Articles

Zea, Leopoldo. "¿Bondad norteamericana e ingratitud mundial?" In *América en la conciencia de Europa.* Mexico: Los Presentes, 1955.
_____ . "Dialéctica de la conciencia en México." in *La filosofía como compromiso.* Mexico: Tezontle, 1952.
_____ . "El puritanismo en la conciencia norteamericana." In *América en la conciencia de Europa.* Mexico: Los Presentes, 1955.
_____ . "El sentido de responsabilidad en el mexicano." *La filosofía como compromiso.* Mexico: Tezontle, 1952.
_____ . "La conciencia del hombre en la filosofía." In *Introducción a la filosofía.* 3rd ed. Mexico: Imprenta Universitaria, 1967.
_____ . "Norteamérica en la conciencia hispanoamericana." In *La filosofía como compromiso.* Mexico: Tezontle, 1952.
_____ . "Ortega el Americano." In *Esquema para una historia de las ideas en Iberoamérica.* Mexico: Imprenta Universitaria, 1956.

INDEX